THE
BIG PERUVIAN
COOKBOOK

THE
BIG PERUVIAN
COOKBOOK

100 DELICIOUS TRADITIONAL RECIPES FROM PERU

MORENA CUADRA
WITH MORENA ESCARDÓ

Skyhorse Publishing

Skyhorse Publishing books may be purchased in bulk at special discounts for sales promotion, corporate gifts, fund-raising, or educational purposes. Special editions can also be created to specifications. For details, contact the Special Sales Department, Skyhorse Publishing, 307 West 36th Street, 11th Floor, New York, NY 10018 or info@skyhorsepublishing.com.

Skyhorse® and Skyhorse Publishing® are registered trademarks of Skyhorse Publishing, Inc.®, a Delaware corporation. Visit our website at www.skyhorsepublishing.com.

10 9 8 7 6 5 4 3 2

Library of Congress Cataloging-in-Publication Data is available on file.

Cover design by Mona Lin
Photos by Morena Cuadra
iStockphoto credit: pg ii, vi, 3, 4, 5, 6, 7, 8, 9, 10, 11, 21

Print paperback ISBN: 978-1-5107-3841-6
Ebook ISBN: 978-1-5107-3786-0

Printed in China

Dedication

To my son, Eduardo Escardó, with all
my love.

And to Fátima and Joaquín Escardó,
my grandbabies, who fill my life with
so much love and joy.

CONTENTS

ACKNOWLEDGMENTS

The making of a cookbook involves a communal effort in which many people contribute in more than one way. This book is no exception, and I would like to thank everyone at Skyhorse Publishing, and in particular Tony Lyons, for giving us the opportunity of doing what we love: creating books! Many thanks to Kristin Kulsavage, our editor on this project. It has been a pleasure to work with you throughout this process.

Special thanks and love to Rob Trehy, who made this book possible, and who is constantly encouraging us with cheerful enthusiasm. Thank you for being our official English language proofreader at late hours of the night, and for all the gourmet grilled cheese sandwiches you cooked for us when working tirelessly to meet deadlines.

Thanks to my baby brother, Chef Roberto Cuadra, for sharing with us delicious ideas, recipes, and photos from your wonderful Peruvian restaurant in San Salvador. Your invaluable help and talent has been a key factor in the making of this book, and we consider it to be yours too.

My deepest love and gratitude to my cousins Carolina and Oscar Alvarez, who were part of this, and other previous adventures, since day one. It was a blessing to have the chance to work for several weeks in your beautiful and fully equipped kitchen overlooking the forest. Your home is a cook´s—and a writer´s—dream. Working there has been inspiring and relaxing, and I couldn´t have found a better place for photo shooting my dishes. Thanks for your friendship, continuous love, support, and generous hospitality.

All my gratitude to my dear Peruvian friends and talented chefs, Ximena Llosa, Flavio Solórzano, Paola Cubas, and Hajime Kasuga, for sharing their unique recipes, first in our blog, and now in this book. A big thank you to Manuel Villacorta too, for his creative and nutritious recipes, and all his insights about Peruvian superfoods. You guys rock!

I would like to thank my lovely daughter-in-law, Antonella Delfino, who is now part of Peru Delights, and constantly shares with us her family's kitchen gems and the beautiful pictures she takes of them. While working on this book, Antonella gave birth to my first granddaughter, Fátima, the most beautiful baby in the whole world.

Thanks, as always, to Alex Smith, Rachel Bowen, and Hector Escardó, for your first-class technical support, without which we wouldn't be here. And many thanks to the super talented Andrea Franco Batievsky, from Nuhr Studio, for her love and beautiful videos.

Thanks to Charles Lyons for his generous support and friendship, and for bringing Peru Delights to life in his Bright Leaf Pictures videos. Thanks to our fellow Latina bloggers, for their friendship, and for helping us become better bloggers, writers, and businesswomen every day. And a warm and special thank you to all my Peruvian friends and family, who constantly amaze me with their love and support.

Thanks to all PeruDelights.com's readers and followers, many of whom have become real-life friends. It is an honor to share our recipes with all of you, to interact through social media, and to get your kind and encouraging emails all the time. We wouldn't be here if it wasn't for you.

And to my angel of love, Morena Escardó, who every single day teaches me something new. Having the chance to work with you is a dream come true. I love you with all my heart.

INTRODUCTION

The story of Peruvian food through the centuries is a delightful tale full of drama that I, as a modern Scheherazade, would love to share with you in this book. So let me set aside both the glorious and the painful sides of our history first, and focus only on the evolution of flavors that have become the core of our interesting gastronomy.

What makes Peruvian cuisine so enticing and wherein lies its huge attraction? I believe the reason behind its massive popularity are the European, African, and Asian flavors and techniques that have been adopted and blended with the local traditions and ingredients. Our cuisine takes pride in being open and flexible with the food of other countries, and this is why we quickly transform every foreign influence into a complex fusion of foods that burst with taste and soul.

Peruvians have been blessed to live in a country that contains most of the world's micro climates within its varied geography. This allows for a fascinating array of luscious, colorful, nutrient-packed and sometimes funny-looking ingredients available year-round. Take the Amazon forest. This region alone boasts one of the most exquisite biodiversities in the entire world, and is home to all kinds of exotic fruits, vegetables, nuts, and legumes, freshwater fish from the rivers and lagoons, and wild animals that make stunning dishes.

In the Andes, the extremely cold weather is ideal to grow native cereals like quinoa, amaranth, *cañihua*, and our beloved giant kernel corn. More than 3,000 varieties of potatoes grow in this part of the country, alongside tubers like *maca* (known as the Peruvian ginseng), *olluco, oca,* and *mashua.* This is the land of llamas, alpacas, and all their relatives, which you can see running free up in the mountains, or turned into sturdy dishes cooked in clay pots with chili peppers and black mint. Vibrant pink trouts from local rivers, and frogs from Huancayo´s lakes are freshly caught and cooked in the moment, the latter sometimes turned into a soup famous for its invigorating properties.

The coast has a completely different weather from these two regions, and as such, its gastronomy is also a completely different animal, both figuratively and literally. This is the kingdom of the Pacific Ocean, a fish and seafood paradise where you will find fresh *cebiches* and *tiraditos* in every corner. The cold water current that runs along the Peruvian coast creates the perfect environment for sea critters to thrive, and for us to thrive on them. And although most of the coast is a desert, there are many small valleys in the river's estuaries where farmers grow countless vegetables and fruits sold daily in the city markets.

With this background, it's easy to understand why our gastronomy is what it is today, and is finally taking the world by storm. In this book you will find a selection of some of our favorite preparations for an assortment of comforting dishes that are considered everyday food in Peruvian homes. We also have added a few creative highlights just for fun. After all, that is what Peruvian food is all about: being open to experimentation and to change, without losing its essence. For the most part, the recipes you will find here will be easy to make and (we think) extremely tasty. We hope you feel the same way, and you learn a few new dishes that will become a part of your life in the kitchen.

Buen provecho!

PERUVIAN FOOD IN HISTORY

Our Roots

Once upon a time Peru was a vast empire that covered most of South America. Despite this land's unbelievable biodiversity, Peruvian food was mostly Andean food, with a few highlights from the coast and the Amazon jungle.

Many of the ingredients known and used today in most parts of the world, considered the most basic and indispensable players in people's diets (like potatoes, tomatoes, corn, and chili peppers), are native to Peru. The ancient Peruvian man domesticated these crops and improved their quality with natural methods, making them resistant to plagues and disease, weather and pests. To us, these were abundant from the beginning of our history, and have never lost their place as staples of our diets.

The Incas, and the cultures before them, put all their efforts in preserving the copious supply of food the *Pachamama* (mother nature) provided them. These people mastered the crafts of smoking, drying, and salting food. In the Andes, they took advantage of the inhospitable temperatures to freeze-dry potatoes and meats to use in times of scarcity. At the same time, they built storage spaces in the mountains, similar to barns, in such a form that cereals were protected from insects and humidity, yet received the right amount of cold air to keep them fresh. Thanks to their intelligence, understanding of agriculture, and innovative methods, food in this empire was bountiful, and the word *famine* was probably not even in their vocabulary.

The cooking methods were simple. They never fried, but instead roasted, toasted, and cooked food using hot stones or baked it in underground ovens. They seasoned their dishes with salt (in the form of a rock that they would add to their clay pots, or by licking the rock while they ate), abundant chili peppers, and lots of Andean herbs such as *huacatay* (black mint), which imparted their intense taste to soups and stews.

Thanks to their mostly vegetarian diet dense with ingredients that are now considered "superfoods" around the world, Peruvians were healthy and strong. They didn´t eat eggs or milk, and meat was not an everyday ingredient for them, but generally eaten in times of celebration. Potatoes, quinoa, *kiwicha* (amaranth), *tarwi, cañihua*, chili peppers, and corn, were, and still are, a few of their daily basics. Sugar was unknown, but they used honey as an occasional treat. They sparingly enjoyed fresh and dried llama meat, *cuy* (guinea pig), and every now and then, fish.

It's hard to believe that fresh fish was brought from the Pacific Ocean to Cusco every day for the Inca's dinner. Although it seems like an impossible task, it was achieved thanks to the famous runners of the empire (called *chasquis*), who were in charge of the transportation of fish and other items that needed to be transported throughout the vast empire. Despite the altitude, lack of communication, and large distances, these men always got to their destination—and they ran as fast as the wind!

The Arrival of the Spanish Conquistadors

The arrival of the Spanish brought new ingredients and foods to America for the first time, along with Moorish women who quickly made their way to Peruvian kitchens with recipes from their homeland. These women were the wives, lovers, or cooks of many Spanish men, and they immediately started adapting their Arab-Spanish dishes until they were barely recognizable, making good use of all the new ingredients this land had to offer. These women are the reason rice pudding, stuffed potatoes, and *alfajores* exist in Peru, among many other dishes, particularly sweets.

Europe also became the recipient of a myriad of native Peruvian fruits, vegetables, and cereals. Tomatoes, for example, were used to decorate hats and gardens in European homes, as well as potatoes, which were grown for their beautiful purple flowers, but were considered too dangerous to eat (they were believed to be poisonous and diabolic). Many years went by before people tried these crops and fell in love with them.

While all this culinary exchange and fusion was taking place, Andean soups and stews also changed forever with the addition of cheese and milk (two ingredients previously considered taboo), with the growing popularity of beef, lamb, and pork, which became the "new meat," and with all the other foreign flavors and techniques that the natives were now exposed to. Both cultures (Peruvian and Spanish) enriched themselves when they found each other, and this was only the beginning of a delicious evolution.

A Food Obsession

I have a fascination with the life and the culinary practices in vogue during the viceroyalty in Peru, and I have eagerly devoured many books on the subject, especially the ones written by food historian Rosario Olivas Weston, whose expertise in Peruvian gastronomy is astounding.

For centuries Lima was a sophisticated city, the center of the Viceroyalty of Peru, where the most important events of the area took place. The city was small—starting with 50 inhabitants and growing from there—but it was beautiful and had a bursting and vibrant commercial, cultural, social, and political life. Travelers from all over the world loved to journey to Lima and enjoy the charm of this cosmopolitan city and its people.

At the time, Lima, as well as other important cities in the country, had a great amount of European inhabitants. Life was quiet and one could even say people's lives revolved around food, as they loved to eat copious amounts of delicious and varied dishes several times a day, especially when guests visited, which was (and still is) frequent.

Social Life

Social life was intense, and constant gatherings and celebrations were held on a daily basis. In fact, Peruvians were always partying and didn´t need a reason to celebrate, and this has been inherited for generations and still goes on today. Every wealthy household had large brigades of servants and cooks to manage the social activities, because the enormous houses with several living rooms, bedrooms, and gardens were extremely high-maintenance.

The kitchens had several cooks and helpers who worked incessantly to provide the constant food supply required from morning to evening. Remember that at the time there were no electric blenders or mixers, no gas stoves or electric ovens. Everything had to be made by hand, and the food was cooked over an open fire. Tough work, I'm sure, but the results must have been excellent, as is usually the case when things are cooked slowly, and from scratch.

According to historians, there were five regular meals every day, as follows:

Breakfast, at 9 a.m.
Lunch, at 3 p.m.
Dinner, at 10 p.m.
"Once" in Spanish (or "eleven" in English), was the time for drinking *aguardiente* (liquor). *Aguardiente* has eleven letters, hence the name.
Finally came the time for *agasajo*, which meant having a cup of hot chocolate, with pastries and cakes on the side, of course. Today we also have a name for that meal, usually enjoyed in the middle of the afternoon. It's called *lonche*.

With a tight food schedule like this, I imagine these people ate all day long! Rumor has it that *Limeñas* (girls from Lima), were famous for having voracious appetites, and for being coquettish and accepting invitations to dine with several gentlemen—not at the same time, of course. The story goes on to tell that these men were always shocked when they realized the amount of food these ladies could gobble up when invited.

Lima: The Garden City

If you take into account the fact that Lima was surrounded by countless farms and orchards, and every home had a garden that produced fresh herbs, fruits, and vegetables, it's easy to imagine how tasty and varied the diet was. People regularly consumed good amounts of protein, cereals, legumes, and particularly sweets. *Limeños* also loved fish and seafood, as is to be expected in a city bordered by the ocean. When it came to eating meat, they didn't favor just one type, but had a variety of hen, native duck, cow, goat, lamb, alpaca, llama, rabbit, and guinea pigs. Potatoes were obviously abundant, as well as other native vegetables and legumes like lima beans, corn, squash, and tomatoes. Food was seasoned with plenty of chili peppers and local herbs.

Papaya, cherimoya, and granadilla, were among the favorite fruits of the time, together with never before seen figs, melons, peaches, and oranges, which were all the rage for the novelty factor. Grapes were brought to Peru by the Spanish Marqués de Carabantes, and gained immediate popularity. This crop adapted very well to Peruvian soil, and it started being used to make wine and *Pisco*, our national spirit. The latter was exported to Spain and became one of the most important sources of income of the Viceroyalty.

Feasting 24/7

What dishes were popular in colonial households? Peruvians were very fond of hearty soups, stews, and huge corn puddings filled with beef. As side dishes, large platters containing boiled corn and potatoes were served on the table, and diners were expected to help themselves to several pieces of each to accompany their entrées.

Before dessert, they ended the savory meal with another dish they loved: the famous *empanada*. But this was not a small, regular, hand-size empanada like the ones we buy in bakeries today. The dish I'm talking about was a gigantic pie that needed to be carried by several servants from the kitchen to the dining room. Guests always took home big portions of this course, perhaps because they were already stuffed with food when the *empanada* made its glorious entrance.

After the meal itself, all kinds of sweets (*maná, polvorones, manjar blanco*) and desserts appeared on the table. Countless jars of water, fruit beverages and juices, liqueurs, and wines were strategically distributed around the table. After dinner, "la jarana" (a creolle party) began with the strumming of a guitar and a *cajón* (drum seat), and people enjoyed themselves, sipping wine, singing, and dancing until past midnight.

Street Vendors

Life in the city was marked by street vendors who offered all kinds of foods, always at the same time.

People didn´t need to watch their clocks to know what time it was because it was enough to hear the street cry of each vendor to know the answer. The non stop parade went like this from dawn till dusk:

6 a.m.: The milk woman

7 a.m.: Herbal teas and *chicha*

8 a.m.: Cakes and sour milk

9 am: The woman selling *sanguito* (a custardy dessert made with corn flour and molasses syrup) and *choncholí* (innards)

10 a.m.: Tamales

11 a.m.: Melons and sweet confections

12 a.m.: *Empanadas* and fruits

1 p.m.: Desserts like rice pudding, and *alfajor*

2 p.m.: *Causa, humitas*, and the *picarones* lady

3 p.m.: More sweets and *anticuchos* (Peruvian kebabs)

4 p.m.: The woman selling *picantes* (stews), and the man with the walnut *piñita* (slow-cooked nut sweet)

5 p.m.: Flower time, and *caramanducas* (bread rolls)

6 p.m.: Medicinal roots and cookies

7 p.m.: The ice cream guy, and the wafer seller

8 p.m.: Candy, *mazamorra*, and *champus*

9 p.m.: The sacristan walked all over the city requesting alms for the souls trapped in the purgatory

This daily display of food ran parallel to the many food joints, cafés, bakeries, elegant restaurants, and food stalls spread all around Lima.

Praying and Cooking

As you can see, colonial life was deeply attached to food. In the convents all around the cities, nuns were famous for making the best desserts, cookies, and candies in the country. They sold them to the public being the equivalent of modern-day catering businesses, and their desserts were requested for parties and every important social gathering that ever took place. Cooking was the nuns' main activity, and their expertise in the trade was very profitable for the convents.

Not long ago, one could still go to the convents to order elaborate cakes to celebrate religious milestones such as first communions and baptisms, or simply to eat at home with friends. In recent years, the competition has become too great for nuns to keep up. Large caterers, bakeries, and grocery stores now prepare most of the sweet delicacies made once only by nuns.

The Italians

For many decades, the best grocery stores in the country were owned by Italian immigrants, who became famous for the quality of the ingredients they sold. On the other hand, stores owned by Peruvians were considered by many as dirty and low class, carrying cheap and ordinary produce. Then Italians transformed their stores into small cafés, offering coffee, Italian dishes, pastries, and breads. They were hardworking people, and the locals admired and respected them, making them their favorite vendors of specialty products.

Italians were the creators of many famous bakeries, ice cream and chocolate factories, and *trattorias*, especially when a larger number of them came to Peru at the end of the nineteenth century. Their satisfying food won the people's hearts, and some of their dishes were transformed to fit Peruvian tastes and adopted by every home cook. This is why you can now find *tallarines rojos* (pasta in tomato sauce), and *tallarines verdes* (pasta with pesto sauce), in every household, on a regular basis. Minestrone became *menestrón*; and panettone became *panetón*. This is Peru's most popular Christmas treat.

Other Important Influences

African

The way African slaves came to our country was sad and unfair, but sometimes amazing things come from the greatest adversity. These men taught Peruvians how to make the most of their scarcity by creating mouthwatering dishes out of the scraps of food they got from their masters. The creativity of these cooks is still revered by all of us, and many of their creations became top-selling classics of Peruvian cuisine. *Sangrecita, tacu tacu,* and *chapanas and frejol colado* are among our countless dishes with African roots.

French
There was a time, after the independence from Spain, that Peruvians turned to France for cultural guidance, and wanted to adopt its sophisticated ways. This was a natural reaction, as they wanted to distance themselves from the Spanish. To achieve this, they started to emulate the food and the manners of French aristocrats. These practices were most notorious among the high class.

As a consequence of this, French food, pastries, and desserts became fashionable, and many French restaurants opened their doors to the public. To this day, bavarois and mousse are made in every possible flavor, and are among the most popular desserts, eaten in many homes on a daily basis.

Chinese
When Chinese laborers came to our country to work for the country's elite in estates, they had contracts that specified what kind and amount of food they were going to receive every month. They were able to keep eating rice and other Chinese ingredients, which allowed them to continue cooking their traditional dishes.

Peruvians were initially suspicious of these unfamiliar men who ate eccentric foods. But Chinese immigrants soon started opening little grocery stores that grew to become what we called *fondas*, or tiny restaurants selling only Chinese food. At the beginning their customers were Chinese only, but little by little, Peruvians opened up to the idea and discovered they liked this exotic food. *Chifas* were born.

What is a *Chifa*? It is a Chinese restaurant with a Peruvian infusion, now found in every corner of the country, and always packed with customers looking for appetizing food at reasonable prices. They are one of the most popular places to go with friends or family for special occasions or during the weekend.

Japanese

Japanese immigrants were very poor when they arrived in Peru, but they became small business owners in just a few years. Many decades had to pass before Peruvian chefs turned to them and learned a thing or two about their food. As you probably know by now, we adopted some of it as ours. The new way of making cebiche on the spot, instead of marinating it for hours in advance, became a hit around the world. Tiradito, with finely cut slices of fish similar to sashimi, was here to stay.

10 WAYS TO EAT LIKE A PERUVIAN

1. Make white rice (with plenty of garlic) your side of choice. Don't be shy. Feel free to accompany absolutely every dish with it. Tons of it.

2. Eat cebiche only during the day. Savoring this raw fish dish at night is taboo, as the fish is no longer at peak freshness.

3. Your dish is not complete unless it has salsa criolla and/or a fried egg on top (a breaded steak works too). Sturdy appetites need large portions. The larger the better.

4. Thirsty? A large glass of cold chicha morada is a must. This drink will go perfectly with breakfast, lunch, dinner, dessert, and the list goes on. It's always a good time to drink some homemade chicha.

5. Keep your ají sauces close at all times. Peruvian food tends to be spicy, but we can't get enough of it. Add extra chili sauce to your food whenever possible. Sweating is a sign that you're doing it right.

6. The dimming light of the afternoon calls for a sweet treat and a hot beverage. Feel free to indulge your sweet tooth during this Peruvian tea time called *el lonche*. Better if you do it while you catch up on the latest gossip with old friends.

7. Never start a meal without sharing a few *piqueos* first. These shared nibbles can be hot, cold, or both. Don't get carried away or you won't have any space left for the rest of your meal.

8. Get creative with your food and mix and match all the dishes you want in one plate (this works really well with leftovers). Don't be intimidated by strange combinations such as cebiche and tallarines verdes. Any combination is acceptable!

9. A light breakfast is for wimps. Dump the cereal and scrambled eggs on toast, and bring out the real food: tamales, pan con chicharrón, aguadito, or any other entrée you feel like having. After all, this is the most important meal of the . . . morning.

10. Start your meal with a *"Provecho!"* Everything will taste better after you say it.

LIFE IN THE MARKETS

The markets found all over Peru are magical places where customers can find everything they are looking for, whether it be fresh produce, seafood, groceries, crafts, or any other item. I see these as mini versions of Persian markets, loud and crowded, with thunderous music playing on several radio outlets, and continuous chatter and laughter in every stall.

Everywhere you turn, these food havens display endless varieties of fruits and vegetables from the small valleys in the coast, from the Andes, and from the lush Amazon jungle. The varied geography offers an unbelievably large variety of produce throughout the whole year, most of it fragrant, juicy, seasonal, and perfectly ripe. I always have a great time finding new ingredients and realizing how much I still have to discover about this country's natural wealth. Visiting these markets feels like being at a playground where you're constantly learning new names and getting to know all kinds of exciting flavors and textures.

There are stalls with every kind of artisan cheese, or fresh and dried beans and legumes; spice corners carrying cinnamon sticks more than three feet long; some sellers sell only Chinese ingredients; others specialize in sweets or dried fruits and nuts.

Fishmongers are among the most popular sellers in the markets, so skilled that they clean and cut whole

fish in a snap, while giving you suggestions on how to cook or season the particular kind of fish or shellfish you are taking home. You can ask for the fillets, together with their bones and heads, which most fishmongers recommend for making flavorful soups, broths, and stews.

These men will also tell you what kind of fish is best for cebiche, and which is better for deep frying, or to bake in a bath of *chicha de jora*, beer, wine, or Asian sauces. In many *mercados* fishmongers even make cebiche in front of their customers who eagerly wait in line for a taste of their skillfully prepared appetizer.

Casero is a key word you need to learn when going grocery shopping in Peru. It literally means "homey," and it's what we call the merchants and also what they call us, their clients. Isn't that funny? Market *caseros* always have a good time getting to know their customers, and they put a lot of effort into selecting the best produce for them. They will touch and smell every fruit and veggie to give you the exact point or ripeness you requested, and they even give you a *yapa* (extra) for free. This usually consists of a little bit more of what you´ve already bought, or a small bunch of herbs that will complement the dish you told them you are going to cook. You can even receive some delicious fruits in season. Don't be shy and request your *yapa* if your *casero* forgets to offer it!

The talent of some *caseros* goes beyond the realm of cooking. Chances are you will find the "natural medicine *caseros*" selling herbs, roots, and seeds used for every ailment you can imagine. *Sangre de grado*, for ulcers; *chancapiedra*, for kidney stones (translation: "stone crasher"); *grama* (grass) and *cola de caballo*

(horse tail), if you need a powerful diuretic. *Uña de gato* (cat's claw), to reduce tumors. Extra bitter *hercampuri*, to lose any unwanted pounds. They also sell *ruda* for good luck and to attract prosperous and abundant business. The usual recommendation is to carry a sprig of this smelly herb in your wallet to make sure it's always overflowing with money.

The most knowledgeable of *caseros* even give their customers natural beauty secrets. They suggest, for example, that you wash your hair with *champus*, an oval fruit with pale and hairy green skin, used as shampoo in the Andes. One of my lifelong *caseras* swears that if you do this, your hair will be as clean and shiny as if you washed it with the most expensive shampoo. Another natural product used is fresh aloe vera gel. I haven´t tried these two beauty methods yet, but generations of Andean women with strong, shiny, black hair, may be enough proof that they are indeed very effective.

Speaking of the Andes, the markets in that part of the country have their own particularities that distinguish them from coastal or Amazonian *mercados*. Bread is an important part of the scene, with huge stalls carrying a large variety of local breads. *Chaplas, chutas, guaguas, tres puntas* . . . all of these are mostly made with whole wheat flour and other wholesome flours, such as quinoa, potato, sweet potato, barley, amaranth, and corn. These breads are a real treat on their own, and even better if filled with mashed avocado, or accompanied by any kind of Andean cheese.

These regional markets also carry beautiful clay pots that can be used for cooking or just to decorate the kitchen or the house. They are hand made, and very

practical to use. Most people in the Andes still cook in these pots today, and this is actually considered a healthier way to cook than using metal pots such as the toxic aluminum ones. Woven baskets, dolls, and countless other objects for the house are very common in these places too.

I'm trying my best to describe the wide diversity of products that each market in Peru has to offer, but let me tell you, this is not an easy task. I hope this chapter gives you at least an idea of what they are like. But whatever you can get from reading about it won't compare to actually spending a few hours in one of these places. All your senses will be awakened.

If you have been to Peru, these photos will be a colorful déjà vu of what you probably experienced. And if you are not personally acquainted with our country yet, I hope this helps you make up your mind to start planning a visit. Our *mercados* are exciting showcases of Peru´s biodiversity, and visiting them is an unforgettable experience.

GETTING STARTED

- Plan ahead when making any of these recipes. Read the recipe from start to finish, checking if you have the right ingredients and/or equipment to make it.

- A cook is as good as the ingredients he has. Buy the best ingredients you can afford, whether it's vegetables, fruits, or any kind of meat. Be particularly careful when buying seafood. Peruvians use only the freshest fish and seafood available, but of course we have the huge advantage of being next to the ocean.

- When using fresh chili peppers, toasting and blanching them will tame the heat while leaving the flavor intact. If all you can find is *ají* paste, start with a small amount and keep tasting it as you add more. These tend to be hotter than their fresh counterparts, so be cautious.

- Some recipes require a little previous preparation (*mise en place*). Prepare the doughs, marinate the meats, wash, peel, and chop everything you will need before starting. Line them in the order you are going to use them to make your life easier when cooking.

- Taste the dish at different stages of the preparation and season accordingly. Feel free to make all the seasoning changes you consider necessary, as there is nothing worse than bland food.

- Vegetarian or vegan versions can be made of most of our dishes. Be adventurous and experiment!

- Stick as much as possible to the first instructions given. Once you know how each recipe turns out and how the dish should look and taste like, you can bring in your own creativity and improvise. Remember that no recipe is written in stone. For us, food is a living, breathing entity, infused with the energy of each cook. Put some music on, roll up your sleeves, and have fun!

PIQUEOS AND SANDWICHES

CANCHA SALADA

Makes 6–8 cups

Roasted dried corn has been eaten in Peru for centuries instead of bread. Up in the Andes, farmers and peasants always carry this snack and some firm artisanal cheese with them to have for lunch, especially when traveling. The highly addictive nibble is called *cancha*, and it's usually cooked in a clay pot.

¼ cup vegetable oil
2 pounds chulpe corn (dried corn)
Salt

Cancha is the traditional nosh served in *cebicherías* while waiting for the food to be served, and it's also the perfect complement for a juicy *cebiche*. It also takes the place of the usual peanuts or chips in most bars.

1. Heat the oil in a saucepan over medium heat. Add the dried corn, and stir constantly until it turns golden brown and cracks start to appear on the surface of each kernel.
2. Take off the heat, add salt to taste, and serve.

FRIED YUCCA STICKS WITH FIERY ROCOTO SAUCE

Serves 6

This is one of our easiest, cheapest, and most delectable hors d´oeuvres. We use any excuse to nibble on these *yuquitas fritas* dipped in some of our favorite sauces (*Huancaína, ocopa, rocoto* sauce, *aji amarillo* sauce, and even guacamole!). They will get your appetite going, preferably accompanied by a very cold beer.

½ *rocoto*, ribbed and seeded (canned or frozen is fine)
1 cup cream cheese or diced *queso fresco*
½ cup vegetable oil
Salt and pepper
1 pound yucca, peeled, boiled, and cut in ½–inch-thick sticks
Vegetable oil for frying

1. To make the *rocoto* sauce: Process the *rocoto*, cheese, and vegetable oil, in a blender until creamy or a little chunky if you prefer it this way. Season with salt and pepper. Reserve.
2. Heat 1 inch of oil in a saucepan, and when hot, fry the yucca sticks a few at a time, until golden. Drain on paper towels.
3. Serve with a bowl of *rocoto* sauce to dip.

The secret for finger-licking fried yucca sticks is to boil the yucca in advance, then cool it, cut it, and freeze it for a few days or weeks. When you want to make them, just take the frozen sticks out and fry them without thawing. The result is a creamy yucca, with a golden crispy crust.

AJÍ DE GALLINA MINI TARTLETS

Makes 24

These adorable tartlets—or *hojarascas*, as we call them in Peru—used to be present in every cocktail or dinner party a few decades ago. Despite being so popular in the past, they were eventually forgotten, as more modern nibbles replaced them.

24 baked mini tartlet shells
1 recipe *ají de gallina*
  (p. 149)
12 hard-boiled quail eggs, peeled
24 curly parsley leaves

1. Place about ½ tablespoon of *ají de gallina* in each tartlet.
2. Garnish with ½ quail egg and a small parsley leaf.
3. Serve immediately with cocktails or white wine.

Do not bother baking the tartlets yourself. Buy them ready-made in a good bakery or grocery store. These tartlets are a good way to use up any *ají de gallina*—or any other stews—leftovers. Use this as inspiration to create your own finger foods.

CONCHITAS A LA PARMESANA

Serves 2

This is a traditional hors d´oeuvre, made with bay scallops covered in grated Parmesan cheese, and ran under the broiler for a few minutes. When served, the cheese is bubbling but the scallops remain almost raw. A crowd pleaser!

12 bay scallops in the half shell (see tip box)
Salt and pepper
12 drops Worcestershire sauce
12 drops lime juice
4 tablespoons butter
12 tablespoons Parmesan cheese, grated

If you can't find bay scallops in the half shell, broil them in small ramekins. If you don't find scallops, you can use razor clams.

1. Preheat the broiler.
2. Clean and wash the scallops in the half shell, dry, and season with salt and pepper.
3. Put them in a baking tray and season each one with a drop of Worcestershire sauce and a drop of lime juice. Cover with one tablespoon grated Parmesan cheese, and ½ teaspoon butter.
4. Run under the broiler for about 4 minutes or until the cheese is bubbling and golden brown.
5. Serve immediately, piping hot, with lime slices on the side.

CHOROS A LA CHALACA—MUSSELS CHALACA-STYLE

Serves 4

This fresh appetizer is a great option for a hot summer day. Lightly steamed mussels are topped with a spicy salsa made with crisp red onion, boiled corn, tomato, *rocoto*, and lime juice. Raw bay scallops can be used instead of mussels.

12 mussels
1 cup white wine
½ cup red onion, finely diced
1 tomato, peeled, seeded, and
   chopped
½ cup corn kernels, cooked
1 tablespoon *rocoto*, chopped
   (fresh or jarred)
4 limes
1 tablespoon olive oil
Salt and pepper
1 tablespoon parsley leaves,
   chopped

1. Clean the mussels and remove the beards attached to the shells by pulling them.
2. Put them in a saucepan with the wine, cover, and bring to a boil for 2 minutes. Check to see if all the mussels are open. If any of them remain closed, discard them. Turn off the heat, take out the mussels, and cool.
3. In the meantime, combine the red onion, tomato, corn, *rocoto*, lime juice, olive oil, salt, pepper, and parsley leaves in a bowl.
4. Discard the top shells of the mussels. Top each mussel with a tablespoon of the salsa and some of its juice, and serve immediately, at room temperature.

Only buy mussels when they are very fresh, and heavy for their size, but not too much because they could be full of sand. Buying fresh mussels is the easiest thing to do in Lima, because the rocks by the shore are covered with them. Be very careful not to overcook them, because they will turn into a rubbery disaster.

SHRIMP TEQUEÑOS

Makes 24

Although *tequeños* are native of Venezuela, Peruvians have adopted them as their own, and eat them whenever they get the chance. These fried cheese-filled wonton fingers, served with guacamole sauce, have inspired many new variations in the past few years. Here you have them filled with shrimp and served with *ají amarillo* sauce.

8 ounces shrimp, peeled
2 scallions, finely chopped
1 egg yolk
Salt and pepper
24 wonton wraps (you can get these in many supermarkets, or Chinese grocery stores)
Vegetable oil for deep frying
1 cup mayonnaise
2 tablespoons *ají amarillo* paste (or to taste)
Juice of ½ lime
Salt and pepper

Tequeños can be filled with crab salad, chopped roasted chicken, cheese, vegetables, or even cooked apples with butter and sugar. When it comes to this finger food, sky's the limit.

1. Finely chop the shrimp and combine with scallions, egg yolk, salt, and pepper.
2. Put ½ tablespoon of this mix on one side of the wonton sheet, and roll the sheet around it, leaving a little edge unrolled. To close, wet your finger and pass it along the edge of the wonton sheet, and then finish rolling. Do the same to close the side ends, pressing with your fingers to make sure the dough sticks well.
3. You can do these first steps in advance, cover the uncooked *tequeños*, and keep in the fridge for up to 2 hours. Fry them right before serving.
4. For the sauce, combine mayonnaise with *ají amarillo* paste, lime juice, salt, and pepper.
5. Put ½ cup vegetable oil in a frying pan over medium/high heat, and fry a few *tequeños* at a time, turning them once until they are golden brown.
6. Transfer to a dish covered with paper towels, to absorb the excess oil.
7. Serve immediately with the *ají amarillo* sauce on the side, to dip them in.

PATACONES

Serves 2

In some countries they are known as *tostones*, but in the northern region of Peru, where plantains are abundant and an important part of the daily diet, these tasty fritters are called *patacones*. They are usually eaten as an accompaniment for meat and fish dishes, instead of bread, French fries, or rice.

1 green plantain
1 cup vegetable oil
Salt

Serve *patacones* as a side dish with pork, fish, or even *cebiche*.

1. Cut the tip ends of the plantain. Make a slit along the skin and peel it.
2. Cut the plantain in 1½-inch round slices.
3. Heat the vegetable oil in a small saucepan over medium heat.
4. Add the plantain slices and fry until they slightly change color. Transfer to a chopping board.
5. With the bottom of a cup or a glass, press each plantain slice to flatten it, but be careful not to split it.
6. Fry again over high heat until they are yellow/golden brown.
7. Transfer to a dish covered with paper towels to drain the excess oil.
8. Sprinkle with salt, and serve.

QUINOA EMPANADAS

Makes 36

Empanadas are one of the most popular finger foods in Latin America, and they come in every size and flavor. Quinoa is not the exception, and mixed with cheese, it turns them into an unforgettable snack or hors d'oeuvre.

1 tablespoon butter
1 tablespoon all-purpose flour
1 cup hot milk, plus 2 tablespoons
Salt and pepper
1 bay leaf
1 cup cooked quinoa (different colors will look prettier)
½ cup Fontina cheese, coarsely grated
36 empanada dough sheets
1 egg, white and yolk divided

We recommend you get store-bought empanada dough. If you're into cooking from scratch, however, use our chard tart dough to make them (p. 63).

1. Heat the butter in a small saucepan over medium heat and add the flour, stirring constantly until a paste is formed (about 2 minutes).
2. Add 1 cup hot milk, beating with a wire whisk until smooth. Add the bay leaf, salt, and pepper. Lower the heat to very low and simmer the sauce until slightly thick, stirring occasionally. Taste for seasoning and turn off the heat.
3. Stir in the cooked quinoa and cheese. Cool.
4. Preheat the oven to 350°F.
5. Put about 1 teaspoon of the quinoa mixture in the center of each empanada circle.
6. Wet the tip of your finger or a brush with the egg white, and pass it along all the edges of the dough.
7. Fold in half and seal tightly, using the tines of a fork to press the edges. Repeat with the rest of the dough, and place in a baking sheet covered with Silpat or parchment paper.
8. Combine the egg yolk with 2 tablespoons milk, and brush the top of the empanadas with this mixture.
9. Bake for 35 minutes or until golden brown.
10. Transfer to racks and serve warm.

TRIPLES

Makes 2

Three basic ingredients make this sandwich our favorite: avocado, tomato, and hard-boiled egg. It may not sound like anything special, but you better try it before judging. Together, these three ingredients make the most delicious sandwich we've ever had, and Peruvians simply can't get enough of it.

1 avocado
1 ripe tomato
2 hard-boiled eggs
¼ cup mayonnaise
6 slices white bread
Salt and pepper

Here's a trick to ensure the bright green color of the avocado: after cutting it, place the seed in a glass of water and leave it there. As long as the seed is submerged in water, the avocado will be green. Does this work? You will have to try it to find out.

1. Peel and thinly slice the avocado. Slice the tomato and put in a colander to drain. Slice the hard-boiled eggs.
2. Spread the mayonnaise on a slice of bread. Put a layer of avocado and another of tomato on top, and sprinkle with salt and pepper.
3. Spread mayo on both sides of another slice of bread, and put this on top of the tomato.
4. Top with a layer of hard-boiled egg slices, and season with salt and pepper.
5. Spread one last slice of bread with mayo on one side, and put that side down, on top of the egg.
6. Cut each sandwich in half and serve.

BUTIFARRAS

Serves 6

Italian immigrants introduced Peruvians to artisan smoked hams, giving birth to the one used to make this sandwich, called *jamón del país* (country ham). This community was also involved in Pisco production, so there has always been a close relationship between both products. If you travel to Peru, stop by any of the traditional Pisco bodegas, and you´ll probably find yourself eating a *butifarra* along with your drink. Living abroad, Antonella Delfino sometimes uses smoked turkey ham.

6 medium ciabatta rolls
1 cup mayonnaise
1 tablespoon mustard
1 tablespoon *ají amarillo* paste
6 leaves iceberg lettuce
¾ pound *jamón del país* (or any ham)
Salsa criolla (p. 79)

1. Preheat the oven to 300°F.
2. Heat the bread for 5 minutes and cut lengthwise.
3. In a small bowl, combine the mayonnaise, mustard, and *ají amarillo* paste, and spread on the bread.
4. Put a lettuce leaf in the bread (you may have to fold it or break it), then add the ham, and finally top with *salsa criolla*.

Jamón *del país* used to be made at home, by seasoning a boned pork leg with salt, pepper, garlic, *achiote*, cumin, dry oregano, and lard, and cooking it for several hours. But thankfully, you can conveniently buy it in many stores nowadays.

ASADO SANDWICH

Serves 6

This comforting sandwich is made when there are roast beef leftovers from lunch or dinner. Whatever is left has two basic fates: it either goes in the freezer to be enjoyed someday in the future, or it goes into a scrumptious sandwich. I love this recipe, given to us by Antonella Delfino.

6 ciabatta rolls or French bread
12 *asado* slices (p. 145)
¾ cup mayonnaise
1 tablespoon *ají amarillo* paste
Salsa criolla **(p. 79)**

You may add lettuce leaves, tomato slices, and avocado to this sandwich.

1. Preheat the oven to 300°F.
2. Heat the bread for 5 minutes and cut lengthwise.
3. In the meantime, heat the beef with its juices in a saucepan over medium heat, until it is warm.
4. In a small bowl, combine the mayonnaise and *ají amarillo* paste. Spread on the bread.
5. Put the meat slices (with no sauce) inside the rolls, and top with *salsa criolla*.
6. Serve immediately.

SANGUCHÓN

Serves 1

A *sanguchón* (big sandwich) is the late-night snack of choice for Lima's party people. It's a sandwich filled with lettuce, tomato, a burger, grilled cheese slices, a fried egg, string potatoes, and several sauces and dressings. It may sound like a total bomb, especially so late at night, but it´s reinvigorating after spending many hours on the dance floor. This is a vegetarian rendition of this voluptuous meal.

2 slices of bread
½ tomato, thinly sliced
1 lettuce leaf
1 slice of cheese
1 fried egg
Salt and pepper
1 teaspoon mayonnaise
1 teaspoon mustard
1 teaspoon ketchup
½ teaspoon *ají amarillo* paste

1. Grill or toast the bread, with the cheese on top of one of the slices.
2. Top one of the slices with tomato, lettuce, the fried egg, salt, pepper, and all the sauces.
3. Cover with the other slice, and serve.

You can make a vegan version of this sandwich by leaving out the cheese and egg, and adding a vegan burger instead.

GLUTEN-FREE QUINOA CORNBREAD

Makes 16 two-inch squares

Manuel Villacorta, author of the book *Peruvian Power Foods: 18 Superfoods, 101 Recipes, and Anti-aging Secrets from the Amazon to the Andes,* gave us this delicious recipe to share in this book. It was created to accompany the quinoa and pichuberry chili on page 155.

1 cup water
½ cup quinoa
¼ cup olive oil
1½ cups cornmeal (medium-ground)
½ cup quinoa flour
1½ teaspoons baking powder
1 teaspoon salt
¼ cup sugar
2 eggs
1¼ cups milk

Use any color of quinoa you prefer or have at hand. Regular cream-colored quinoa will go unnoticed in the batter, but red or black quinoa (or a combination) will make this cornbread colorful and fun. Besides boosting its nutritional value, quinoa will impart an interesting texture to this bread.

1. Bring water to a boil in a saucepan over medium heat. Add the quinoa and lower the heat to a simmer. Put the lid on and cook until all the water is absorbed (about 15 minutes). Fluff with a fork and set aside to cool.
2. Preheat the oven to 375°F.
3. Place the olive oil in an 8-inch square baking dish, and put inside the oven.
4. Put the cornmeal, quinoa flour, baking powder, salt, and sugar in a large bowl. Whisk to combine and stir in the cooled quinoa.
5. In another bowl, combine the eggs and milk.
6. Add the wet ingredients to the dry ingredients and whisk to combine.
7. Carefully remove the baking dish from the oven and quickly pour the oil into the batter. Stir well.
8. Transfer the batter to the hot baking dish, and bake for 20–25 minutes, until set and golden brown.
9. Let cool slightly before serving.

APPETIZERS

PAPA A LA HUANCAÍNA

Serves 4

If you ask a Peruvian what her favorite sauce is, the answer will probably be the creamy salsa *Huancaína*. Legend has it that a cook created it to accompany the boiled potatoes she sold for lunch to the railway workers in Huancayo, a beautiful city high in the Andes.

½ cup *ají amarillo* paste
2 tablespoons vegetable oil
1 cup evaporated milk
4 soda crackers
8 ounces *queso fresco* (fresh white cheese)
Salt
6 yellow potatoes, boiled and peeled (see tip box)
8 Iceberg or Romaine lettuce leaves
8 Alfonso olives
3 hard-boiled eggs, peeled and cut in slices
4 parsley sprigs

1. Put the *ají amarillo* paste in the blender, add oil and milk, and process with the crackers, *queso fresco*, and salt, until smooth.
2. Cut the potatoes in thick slices (about ½-inch thick).
3. Put 2 lettuce leaves on each plate, some potato slices, and cover with a few tablespoons of the sauce.
4. Garnish with 2 black olives, hard-boiled egg slices, and parsley.

Starchy yellow potatoes are the number one choice when making this traditional dish. Cook them in boiling water until tender, peel them while still hot, and slice them thickly (or use them whole if they're small). If you can't find this kind of potato, use Yukon Gold or Russet.

OCOPA

Serves 4

This is one of the most traditional dishes of our cuisine. The recipe and photo were given to us by celebrity chef Flavio Solorzano. He is the executive chef of the famous restaurant *El Señorío de Sulco*, in Lima, which specializes in Peruvian cooking. Flavio is not only an expert in Peruvian cuisine but he is also a cookbook author and a TV personality.

½ cup toasted peanuts
½ cup red onion, chopped
2 garlic cloves
3 tablespoons *ají mirasol* paste
2 tablespoons *ají amarillo* paste
¼ cup pecans
6 fresh *huacatay* (black mint)
   leaves, or 1–2 teaspoons
   huacatay paste
6 animal crackers
½ cup evaporated milk
½ cup milk
½ cup *queso fresco*, diced
Salt
4 lettuce leaves
1 pound Yukon Gold potatoes,
   boiled and peeled
8 Botija or Alfonso olives
2 hard-boiled eggs, cut in fourths

1. Put the peanuts in a pan, and turn the heat to medium low. Shake the pan gently for a few minutes, until the peanuts are fragrant (do not let them brown). Take off the heat.
2. Roast the onion and garlic in a clean saucepan over medium heat. Turn off the heat and reserve.
3. Process the *ají mirasol, ají amarillo*, onion, garlic, peanuts, pecans, *huacatay*, crackers, evaporated milk, milk, *queso fresco*, and salt, in a blender until smooth. Taste for seasoning and add more salt if needed.
4. In each of four dishes put a lettuce leaf, some potato slices on top, and cover with the sauce.
5. Garnish with 2 Botija olives and 2 egg slices.

Just like *Huancaína* sauce, *ocopa* can be used in countless ways. Turn it into a dip for fried yucca sticks, mini potatoes, or quail eggs; or serve it over pasta, topped with roasted vegetables.

CAUSA

Serves 4

This is a dish that dates back to Incan times, and its original name in Quechua—*Kausay*, which means "what nurtures you"—is proof of it. Incas used to feast on yellow potatoes with salt and ají amarillo. Lime juice was added later, and this delightful potato terrine was born.

6 medium Yukon Gold potatoes
½ cup *ají amarillo* paste
¼ cup vegetable oil
Juice of 3 limes
Salt and pepper
1 can of tuna
¾ cup mayonnaise
1 avocado
4 hard-boiled eggs, sliced
6 Botija or Alfonso olives, sliced
2 tablespoons parsley, chopped
1 tomato, seeded and diced
1 cup giant kernel corn, boiled (or regular white corn)

To make *causa* you can use yucca, sweet potatoes, fava beans, lima beans, taro, or any other vegetable with a starchy texture instead of the classic potatoes. You can also substitute the *ají amarillo* with *rocoto* or roasted bell peppers to give this dish a different color and flavor.

1. Scrub the potatoes and cook in a saucepan with water to cover, for 20 minutes, or until soft but not mushy. Drain and peel while hot, mashing them immediately with a potato masher or a ricer.
2. Add the *ají amarillo* paste, vegetable oil, lime juice, and salt, kneading the potato mixture until all the ingredients are well incorporated. It should be very smooth. Taste for seasoning.
3. Cover the mixture with a kitchen towel and reserve.
4. Combine the tuna and mayonnaise in a bowl.
5. Lightly oil 4 pastry rings. Line the base of the pan with a layer of the potato dough, flattening it out with a spatula. Cover with the tuna mixture and add another layer of potato. Then make a layer of avocado slices, sprinkle with salt and pepper. Add the remaining potato mixture.
6. Cover with plastic wrap and put in the fridge until you want to serve it (you can also serve it immediately).
7. Unmold by running a knife around all the inner edges of the pastry rings, and lift the rings carefully. Garnish with hard-boiled eggs, black olives, parsley, tomato, and corn. (You can choose any mix of these ingredients, or get creative and add your own.)
8. Serve cold.

SOLTERITO

Serves 3

Originally from Arequipa, a beautiful region in the Andes, this refreshing salad is easy and cheap to make, and this is why we love having it as often as possible. There are as many versions of *solterito* as there are cooks in kitchens, and in our case, we love adding quinoa to the recipe for extra texture and a nutritional boost.

1 cup frozen baby fava beans
½ cup red onion, diced
1 cup tomato, seeded and diced
1 cup giant kernel corn, boiled
1 cup *queso fresco*, diced
½ *rocoto* (fresh, frozen, or jarred), and diced (see tip box)
3 tablespoons red or white wine vinegar
3 tablespoons olive oil
Salt and pepper
¼ cup Botija or Alfonso olives, sliced
2 tablespoons chopped parsley
6 lettuce leaves (optional)

1. Cook the fava beans in boiling salted water for 3 minutes. Drain.
2. Combine the fava beans, onion, tomato, corn, *queso fresco*, and *rocoto* in a bowl.
3. Season with vinegar, olive oil, salt, and pepper.
4. Add the parsley and black olives.
5. Serve over lettuce leaves (optional).

Rocoto has the appearance of a sweet and innocent red bell pepper, but beware! It is extremely hot and could make you shed a tear or two. To tame this powerful veggie when it's fresh, you need to remove the seeds and ribs, and rub the inside with sugar. Another effective method is to boil it three times in water with a tablespoon of sugar and vinegar each time, changing the water every time it boils. Substitute with red bell pepper if you cannot tolerate the heat.

TAMALITOS VERDES

Serves 10

These fresh corn and cilantro mini tamales are eaten as a light appetizer or a side dish. They are extremely popular in Peru, especially in the northern coast of the country.

2 pounds white corn, fresh
2 cups cilantro leaves
1 cup spinach (optional)
1½ cups vegetable oil
Salt and pepper
Green corn husks
Salsa criolla **(p. 79)**

If you want to make *humitas* (a different kind of fresh corn tamales), skip the cilantro and spinach and add 1 tablespoon of *ají amarillo* paste to the corn. Fill with a slice of *queso fresco*.

1. Process the corn, cilantro, and spinach in a food processor or a grain grinder until the mixture looks like cooked oatmeal. You can use the blender but the texture could become too liquid, affecting the resulting *tamalitos*.
2. Put the processed corn in a bowl, add oil, and stir gently with a wooden spoon or a spatula, until smooth, about 20 minutes. Season with salt and pepper.
3. Clean the husks with a damp kitchen towel and proceed to make the tamales, by placing 1½–2 tablespoons of corn dough in the center of 2 overlapping husks.
4. Fold the husks around the dough to form a rectangle, fold the tips (ends) and tie with kitchen twine, and reserve. When all the dough has been used, put the remaining husks at the bottom of a wide saucepan.
5. Put the *tamalitos* in a pan with 2–3 cups boiling water, make a layer of husks on top to cover, and cook for 25 minutes. Turn off the heat and let them cool.
6. You can eat the *tamalitos* at once, but they will hold their shape better after a few minutes.
7. Serve 2 *tamalitos* per person, with *salsa criolla* on the side.

CHARD TART

Serves 6–8

We love this chard tart. It is a delicious light lunch, a tasty mid afternoon snack, or even a great breakfast. Serve it warm or cold, with slices of lime on the side.

For the crust:
2½ cups all-purpose flour
½ cup butter
½ cup vegetable shortening
1 teaspoon salt
1 teaspoon sugar
5–6 tablespoons iced water, for blending

For the filling:
2 bunches swiss chard
1 bunch spinach or kale
½ yellow onion, diced
2 garlic cloves, chopped
2 tablespoons vegetable oil
Salt and pepper
¼ teaspoon grated nutmeg
½ cup grated Parmesan cheese
6 eggs
Egg wash (1 beaten egg with 1 tablespoon water)
4 limes, cut in quarters

Before pouring the chard filling over the crust, you can line the base with some thin slices of Edam cheese, for extra flavor and to get a firmer tart.

1. For the crust: Combine the flour, butter, vegetable shortening, salt, and sugar in a food processor. Pulse the mixture until it resembles raw oatmeal. Add 5–6 tablespoons iced water, one at a time, and pulse until a dough forms. Wrap in plastic film or put in a plastic bag and refrigerate for at least 30 minutes. This dough can be kept in the refrigerator for up to 3 days or frozen for up to 3 months.
2. For the filling: Remove the tough veins from the chard. Chop the chard. Do the same with the spinach or kale (trimming and chopping).
3. Rinse the chopped leaves under cold running water and set aside.
4. In a medium-sized saucepan set over medium-high heat, warm the oil and then toss in the onion and garlic. Sauté until tender and translucent, (about 3 minutes). Add the chard and spinach, salt, pepper, and nutmeg. Cook for another 2–3 minutes, stirring. Take off the heat and mix in the grated Parmesan cheese. Taste for seasoning and cool.
5. Preheat the oven to 375°F.
6. Roll half the dough on a floured surface, until it's larger than the baking pan. You will use (a 9-inch springform pan).
7. Transfer to the pan and press gently with your fingers, sticking it to the bottom and sides of the pan, all the way to the edge.
8. Be sure to drain all the juice you can from the leaves before pouring the filling into the pan (otherwise the crust will get soggy).
9. Pour the chard and spinach filling into the pan. Make 6 small crevices in the filling, and break one egg into each one.
10. Roll the rest of the dough, and cover the pie with it, folding the edges to seal the tart.
11. Brush with egg wash and place on the middle rack of the oven. Bake for approximately 45–55 minutes or until the top crust is golden brown.
12. Let cool for about 10–15 minutes before slicing.
13. Serve with lime wedges.

ARTICHOKE TART

Serves 6

The usual way of making this tart is to cover it with a top crust. This time, however, I chose to leave out the extra layer just to enjoy more of the exquisite filling with fewer distractions.

For the crust:
2½ cups flour
½ cup butter
½ cup vegetable shortening
1 teaspoon salt
1 teaspoon sugar
5–6 tablespoons iced water

For the filling:
2 cups baby artichokes or artichoke hearts
1 tablespoon olive oil
3 tablespoons butter
1 garlic clove, minced
½ cup red onion, finely chopped
3 tablespoons flour
3 cups milk
½ cup Parmesan cheese
4 eggs
Salt, pepper, and nutmeg (to taste)

Artichokes are not only beautiful and complex on the outside, but they are also filled with deep inner beauty in the form of nutrition. Peruvians save the water in which artichokes have cooked, and drink it for its liver-enhancing benefits.

1. In a food processor, combine all the ingredients for the crust—except the water—until they acquire the texture of raw oatmeal.
2. Start adding the water, 1 tablespoon at a time, and pulse until a dough forms.
3. Wrap this dough in plastic film and refrigerate for at least ½ hour, and up to 3 days. You can also freeze it for up to 3 months.
4. Preheat the oven to 350°F. When ready, flatten out the dough on a floured surface, with a rolling pin.
5. Line a 9-inch spring form baking pan with dough, and pinch all the surface with a fork.
6. Bake for 10 minutes (you can cover the dough with parchment paper, and put dried beans or chickpeas on top to avoid any bubbles from forming).
7. For the filling: Finely chop the artichokes.
8. Heat the oil and butter in a pan over medium heat. Sauté the garlic and onion, stirring until soft.
9. Turn the heat off and add the flour, whisking constantly to avoid any lumps from forming. Gradually add the milk, and don't stop whisking.
10. When the mixture is smooth, turn the heat back on, and bring to a boil, stirring, until the sauce thickens and becomes creamy.
11. Add the artichoke, cheese, and seasonings, stir well, and take off the heat. Let it cool for 15 minutes.
12. After 15 minutes, beat the eggs with a fork or a hand whisk. Add to the artichoke mixture, and pour over the pre cooked crust. after removing the dried beans and parchment paper.
13. Bake for 40 minutes, remove from the oven, and let cool for 15 minutes before cutting and serving.

PAPA RELLENA— STUFFED POTATO

Makes about 8 large ones or 12 small ones

These mashed potatoes filled with beef and pan-fried are traditionally served as an appetizer. We, however, like having them as an entrée, accompanied with rice and *salsa criolla*. Use chicken, fish, seafood, mushrooms, artichokes, cheese, or soy meat in the filling to make them different every time.

2 pounds waxy potatoes
¼ cup vegetable oil
1 medium red onion, finely diced
2 garlic cloves, minced
1 tablespoon *ají panca* paste (optional)
1 tablespoon tomato paste
1 pound ground beef
1 bay leaf
2 hard-boiled eggs, peeled and chopped
½ cup raisins
½ cup black olives, sliced
Salt and pepper
⅓ cup parsley, chopped
1 cup all-purpose flour
2 eggs, whisked
Vegetable oil for frying
***Salsa criolla* (p. 79)**

If you want to make this vegetarian, follow the recipe steps substituting the meat with vegetarian minced meat, or with chopped portobello mushrooms.

1. Cook the potatoes until tender (about 20 minutes) in a saucepan with water to cover, over high heat.
2. Peel them while hot, and mash them with a potato masher or with a ricer. Season with salt and pepper. Cover with a kitchen cloth and cool to room temperature.
3. To make the filling: Heat the oil in a saucepan over medium heat. Add the onion and garlic, and sauté stirring frequently.
4. When they look transparent, add the *ají panca*, (if you are using this ingredient) and the tomato paste.
5. Add the ground beef, stirring until it changes color. Add the bay leaf and a cup of water, put the lid on, turn the heat to medium-low, and simmer for 15 minutes. Taste for seasoning and turn off the heat.
6. Mix in the chopped eggs, raisins, and black olives. Cool this filling to room temperature.
7. Knead the potatoes for a few seconds with floured hands. Take a portion of the potato mixture (about ¾ cup) and flatten it between your hands, in the shape of a *tortilla*.
8. Put a portion of the beef mixture in the center of the potato circle. Fold the potato around the filling, enclosing it completely and forming a little potato "football."
9. Dip each meat-filled potato football in the whisked eggs, and then roll it in the flour, shaking the excess off. Fry in a pan with hot oil until a thin golden and crusty layer is formed all around the potato.
10. Drain on a dish covered with paper towels and serve immediately with *salsa criolla*.

SHRIMP COCKTAIL

Serves 4

Light, beautiful, and classic, this appetizer has always been at the top of the list of my summer repertoire. The creaminess of the avocado, the silkiness of the colorful sauce, and the freshly caught and lightly cooked shrimp, all contribute to the pleasurable experience of enjoying this easy to make dish.

1 pound shrimp
4 shrimp with heads
  (for garnish)
Salt and pepper
½ cup mayonnaise
2 tablespoons ketchup
1 teaspoon Worcestershire sauce
1 teaspoon brandy (optional)
2 avocados
4 curly parsley sprigs

The dressing in this seafood cocktail is called "Golf" sauce, and it's also ideal to serve with fish fritters, calamari, avocado salad, or even on a hamburger, or accompanying some French fries.

1. Wash the shrimp under cold running water. Peel and discard the peels.
2. Make a cut along the back of the shrimp to discard the veins by pulling them out with the tip of a knife. Wash again.
3. Bring a pan of water with salt to a boil over medium heat. Add the shrimp (including the whole ones), turn the heat to medium low, and simmer for 3 minutes or until they turn pink. Transfer to a bowl to cool.
4. In the meantime, make the sauce by combining mayonnaise and ketchup in a bowl. Stir, add the Worcestershire sauce (and brandy if using it) and reserve. Season with salt and pepper.
5. Peel the avocados, discard the seeds, and cut the pulp in dices.
6. Put ½ avocado in each martini glass—you can use any other serving dish or glass—cover with Golf sauce, and hang the cooked shrimp on the rim of the glass.
7. Garnish with a whole shrimp and a sprig of curly parsley.

QUINOA TABOULEH

Serves 4

Bulgur wheat has been replaced in this refreshing salad by the wonder seed of the Andes: quinoa. It´s super easy to make, so try it!

1 cup quinoa
1 cup water
¼ cup olive oil
¼ cup lemon juice
½ cup fresh mint, chopped
1 cup fresh parsley, chopped
2 garlic cloves, minced
2 tomatoes, chopped
½ cucumber, diced
4 scallions, sliced
Salt (to taste)

For a nice variation of this dish, add 2 cups cooked garbanzo beans and/or 1 cup cooked lentils. This will transform the salad into a complete and balanced meal.

1. Put the quinoa and water in a small saucepan. Bring to a boil over high heat, and then lower to medium heat. When the quinoa is cooked (after about 17 minutes), turn off the heat. If there's any water left in the pan, drain it, and let the quinoa cool.
2. Mix the olive oil, lemon juice, mint, parsley, and garlic in a bowl.
3. Mix the quinoa and chopped tomatoes, cucumber, and scallions. Season with salt.
4. Add the dressing, and mix well.

ANTICUCHOS

Serves 4

These cow heart kebabs have been part of our culinary history for centuries. They are street food at its best, and are usually enjoyed accompanied by traditional Peruvian music, laughter, and dancing.

1 heart of cow or veal (use chicken or beef if you prefer)
½ cup *ají panca* paste
1 tablespoon garlic, finely chopped
¼ cup red wine vinegar
1 tablespoon dried oregano
½ cup vegetable oil
Salt
1 teaspoon ground cumin
2 Russet potatoes, boiled, peeled, and cut in thick slices
2 Peruvian giant kernel corns, boiled, and cut in thick slices
½ cup *ají amarillo* paste mixed with 1 tablespoon chopped scallions and salt

To achieve the best *anticuchos*, season them carefully. You don't want to make them too spicy, because some chili sauces will be served on the side. Cook them briefly, because they become really hard when overcooked.

1. Make sure your butcher cleans and deveins the heart when you buy it. Cut it in 1½-inch squares.
2. In a bowl, combine the *ají panca* paste, garlic, vinegar, oregano, oil, salt, and cumin. Add the heart cubes, cover, and marinate for at least three hours in the fridge.
3. Make a brush with fresh corn husks, to baste the *anticuchos*, or use any brush.
4. Pierce three or four heart pieces onto each bamboo skewer, and grill at medium heat, basting with the marinade, until cooked through (about 3 minutes on each side).
5. Take them off the heat, put on plates, and serve with potatoes, corn, and *ají* sauce.

CHICKEN ANTICUCHOS

Serves 4

A fiery love affair with anticuchos has been going on in the streets of Lima since colonial times. The most famous are made of cow's heart, but sirloin, chicken, veggies, seafood, and lamb variations can also be found. Tender chicken breasts are a great ingredient for these flavorful morsels.

**6 chicken breasts, boned and
  skinned**
Salt and pepper
2 garlic cloves, chopped
2–4 tablespoons ají mirasol paste
1 tablespoon vegetable oil
1 teaspoon dried oregano
Dash of ground cumin
6 potatoes, boiled and peeled

Use mushrooms instead of chicken for a vegetarian version. Whole button mushrooms or diced portobellos are fantastic in these *anticuchos*.

1. Cut the chicken breasts in bite size pieces. Season with salt and pepper, and add garlic, ají mirasol paste, vegetable oil, oregano, and cumin. Cover and marinate in the fridge for two hours.
2. Pierce the chicken pieces with the bamboo skewers, and cook in a hot sauté pan or on the grill, turning after 4–5 minutes, or when golden. Do not overcook the chicken.
3. Meanwhile, cut the potatoes in thick slices and cook in a pan with a little oil, over medium heat, until golden.
4. Put two skewers on each plate, with golden potatoes on the side. A green salad or salsa criolla are great additions to this chicken dish.

ANDEAN CHICKEN FRITTERS

Serves 4

Traditional chicken fritters are covered in quinoa in this recipe to give them an Andean touch. This superfood adds texture to this dish by making it crunchier, and it gives it a beautiful color, which will vary depending on the type of quinoa used.

1.5 pounds skinless chicken breast
Salt and pepper
2 garlic cloves, mashed
2 tablespoons finely chopped
  parsley, divided
1 tablespoon mustard
1 tablespoon lemon juice
1½ cups all-purpose flour
2 lightly beaten eggs
1 cup cooked quinoa
1 cup vegetable oil
1 cup mayonnaise
1 tablespoon *ají amarillo* **paste**
1 tablespoon lime juice
1 tablespoon capers, chopped
Fried plantain strings, to garnish
  (optional)

To make the fried plantain strings, peel a green plantain, and cut thin slices using a vegetable peeler, and then cut to make strings thin like matchsticks. Fry in hot oil for a few minutes, until lightly golden. Drain on paper towels, sprinkle with salt, and serve.

1. Cut the chicken in slices (about 2 inches long and ¾ inch thick).
2. Season with salt and pepper. Add garlic, half the parsley, mustard, and lemon juice. Mix, cover, and marinate in the fridge for one hour.
3. Put the flour in one bowl, the eggs in another one, and the quinoa in a third one.
4. Dip each chicken piece in flour, then eggs, and then quinoa. Put on a plate.
5. Heat the oil in a saucepan over medium heat.
6. Fry the chicken, a few pieces at a time, turning once until golden all around (about 5 minutes). Transfer to a plate covered with paper towels to drain the oil.
7. Combine the mayonnaise, *ají amarillo* paste, lime juice, capers, and the remaining parsley in another bowl. Season with salt and pepper, and stir.
8. Serve the fritters with the sauce on the side and garnish with a few plantain strings.

SALSA CRIOLLA

Serves 2

Onion, *ají amarillo*, cilantro, and lime juice. *Salsa criolla* accompanies most of our dishes, such as *tamales*, sandwiches, and any kind of beans. Make it right before serving to fully enjoy its crispness and vibrant flavor.

½ **medium red onion, finely sliced from top to root**
1 *ají amarillo,* **cut in thin slices (or any other fresh chili pepper)**
½ **bell pepper, thinly sliced (optional)**
2 **tablespoons cilantro leaves, chopped**
Salt and pepper
Juice of 1 lime
1 **tablespoon olive oil**

1. Put the onion in a bowl, cover with ice water, and let rest for 5 minutes. Drain thoroughly.
2. In a bowl, combine the onion, *ají amarillo*, bell pepper, cilantro leaves, salt, pepper, lemon juice, and olive oil. Mix carefully.
3. Use immediately or keep refrigerated up to 1 hour.

When you put onions in ice water they remain crunchy and lose their harsh taste. Season them at the very last minute to keep the onions crisp. If you prefer to enjoy this salsa´s flavor without the heat, use bell peppers instead of *ají amarillo*.

CEBICHES

CEBICHE

Serves 4

Only five ingredients are needed for a good *cebiche*: fish, onion, lime juice, hot chili peppers, and salt. To this basic preparation, you can add anything you want, such as garlic, celery, herbs, and ginger. The possibilities are endless.

1½ pounds flounder fillets, cut in bite-size pieces
1 red onion, cut in fine slices
Juice of 10 limes
2 tablespoons *ají amarillo* paste
1 garlic clove, finely diced
1-inch piece celery stick, finely chopped
Salt
2 tablespoons cilantro leaves, chopped
1 sweet potato, boiled, peeled, and thickly sliced
1 giant kernel corn, boiled in water with 1 tablespoon sugar
4 lettuce leaves

1. Combine the lime juice, ají amarillo paste, garlic, celery, salt, and 1 tablespoon cilantro in a bowl.
2. In another bowl, combine the fish and onion, and wash them together. Drain and season with salt.
3. Add the lime juice mixture to the fish with 5 ice cubes to tame the acidity of the lime. Stir, taste for seasoning, and remove the ice.
4. Serve the cebiche on 4 plates and sprinkle with chopped cilantro.
5. Put a lettuce leaf on the side, and place the corn and sweet potatoes on top of it.

It's important to start with the freshest fish available. If possible, make sure your main ingredient spent the previous night still swimming in open water. Frozen fish is a big and most definite NO when it comes to this minimalistic delicacy.

POWERFUL CEBICHE

Makes 4

Cebiche is one of those dishes with countless variations. This one has all the flavors of the famous Bloody Mary, with tomato juice as the star. A side of fried wonton wraps gives it a beautiful and exotic look, and an unexpected crunchy texture as well.

1 pound shrimp
1 pound calamari, cut into rings
3 cups hot fish stock
1 pound fish fillets
Juice of 10 limes
1 5-ounce can tomato juice
1 ounce Worcestershire sauce
1–2 teaspoons *rocoto* paste
Salt
2 avocados, peeled and sliced
1 cup red onion, finely sliced
1 tablespoon chopped cilantro
4 cilantro sprigs
20 fried wonton wraps

Cut each wonton wrap diagonally. Heat ½ cup vegetable oil in a frying pan over medium heat, and fry the wonton triangles for a couple minutes until medium golden brown. Drain on paper towels. Keep in tightly sealed containers for up to 2 days.

1. Clean the shrimp and calamari and blanch for 2 minutes in boiling fish stock. Drain and cool.
2. Cut the fish in 1 x 1–inch pieces. Put in a bowl and mix with the shrimp and calamari. Season with salt and add lime juice.
3. In another bowl, mix the tomato juice with Worcestershire sauce, *rocoto* paste, salt, and pepper.
4. Combine the tomato mixture with some of the lime juice in which the fish is marinating, and add 4 ice cubes to cool for two minutes. Discard the ice cubes.
5. To assemble the *cebiche*, put 2 avocado slices on each plate. Put ¼ of the *cebiche* on top.
6. Drizzle with ¼ of the tomato sauce.
7. Add chopped cilantro and sliced onion, and garnish with cilantro sprigs.
8. Serve with fried wonton wraps on the side (see tip box).

PASSION FRUIT TIRADITO

Serves 4

Tiradito is a fresh and delicate cross between sashimi and *cebiche*. It is tasty, full of protein, and very low in fat, making it a wonderful option for those trying to avoid fatty meals, or on a low-carb diet.

1 pound white fish fillet
Juice of 5 limes
¼ cup passion fruit juice (it can be frozen)
1 teaspoon *ají amarillo* paste
1 teaspoon diced *ají limo* (or 1 teaspoon *ají limo* paste)
1 garlic clove, grated
½ teaspoon ginger, grated
1 tablespoon olive oil
Salt and pepper
Lettuce leaves
1 sweet potato, cooked and cut in thick slices
¼ cup Peruvian giant corn kernels (or any white kernel)
1 tablespoon black sesame seeds

To make passion fruit juice at home, cut the fruit in half and scoop the pulp into the vase of a blender. Process for 15 seconds on low speed and strain, discarding the black seeds.

1. Thinly slice the fish fillet, wafer thin, like carpaccio. Put the slices on 4 cold plates and sprinkle with salt.
2. In a bowl, combine the lime juice, passion fruit juice, *ají amarillo* paste, diced chili pepper, garlic, ginger, olive oil, salt, and pepper. Pour this juice over the fish.
3. Garnish each plate with a lettuce leaf, and put two sweet potato slices and 1 tablespoon corn kernels on top. Sprinkle the fish with black sesame seeds.
4. Serve immediately.

TIRADITO WITH AJÍ LIMO CREAM

Serves 2

Tiraditos covered with chili pepper creams are all the rage in Peru. Locals never get tired of these creamy and citrusy concoctions that look and feel so elaborate and gourmet, despite the actual simplicity of their preparation. This recipe is a creation of chef Roberto Cuadra.

2 tablespoons red *ají limo* paste
1 tablespoon vegetable oil
1 pound fish fillet
1 teaspoon mashed garlic
Salt and pepper
Juice of 4 limes
2 tablespoons parsley, sliced

To make a different version of this *tiradito* substitute the *ají limo* with *ají amarillo*. This will give the cream a bright yellow color with a floral aroma. You can also use *rocoto* or any other chili pepper.

1. Combine the *ají limo* paste in a bowl with the vegetable oil and blend until smooth.
2. Cut the fish in wafer-thin slices, like carpaccio. Season with mashed garlic, salt, and pepper. Spread the slices on two plates.
3. Combine the *ají limo* cream with the lime juice. Pour over the fish and sprinkle with parsley. Serve immediately.

NIKKEI OYSTER

Makes 1

Hajime Kasuga, one of the best Nikkei chefs, shared this delicate recipe with us. With just a few ingredients, he created this beautiful and sophisticated dish, where the star is the oyster's freshness.

1 fresh oyster
1 tablespoon plus 1 teaspoon shoyu
1 tablespoon plus 1 teaspoon lime
  juice
Pinch of xanthan gum, to thicken
½ scallion, finely sliced, to garnish
A few sprouts, to garnish (optional)

1. Process the shoyu, lime juice, and xanthan gum in a blender.
2. Pour over the oyster, and garnish with scallion slices, and sprouts. Serve immediately.

Make sure the oysters you use are very fresh (your fishmonger should be able to tell you this). If you prefer, use scallops instead of oysters.

SOUPS

PUMPKIN SOUP

Serves 2–4

Fresh vegetable soups are easy to make and comforting during winter. One of our favorites is made with *zapallo loche*, a squash from the northern coast of Peru that is used in many traditional dishes. If you can't find this ingredient, however, any type of squash will do.

2 tablespoons olive oil or butter
½ cup red onion, chopped
2 garlic cloves, chopped
1 peeled and cubed buttercup squash (or the equivalent *zapallo loche*, if you find it)
1 peeled and cubed sweet potato
½ sprig thyme, or any herb you wish to add
Salt and pepper
6 cups water or vegetable stock
Grated or shaved Parmesan cheese to garnish (optional)

For the croutons:
1 garlic clove
3 slices of bread
2 tablespoons olive oil

Regular potatoes are traditionally used for this soup, but we like to add sweet potatoes instead for their sweetness and intense color.

1. Heat the olive oil or butter in a large pan over medium/high heat. Sauté the onion and garlic, stirring constantly until lightly golden.
2. Add the squash, sweet potato, and herbs; season with salt and pepper, and stir well.
3. Add the water or stock, put the lid on, and simmer for 20 minutes or until the vegetables are tender. Turn off the heat, remove the lid, and let cool to lukewarm.
4. In the meantime, cut the garlic in half and rub the bread with it. Then cut the bread in cubes, and drizzle with olive oil. Broil for 5 minutes or until golden and crispy.
5. Process the soup in small batches in the blender, until creamy. Make sure it's not too hot when you do this because it might splash, and you could burn yourself. Put the soup back in the saucepan and taste for seasoning. You may use an immersion blender if you have one.
6. Serve the soup very hot with a few croutons on top, some fresh herbs, and a sprinkle of grated Parmesan cheese.

SPINACH CREAM SOUP

Makes 3

In Peru we love having all kinds of simple vegetable soups. This is a very basic recipe that allows lots of variations. If you substitute the spinach with other veggies, you will have a new cream soup every time. Use asparagus, zucchini, corn, onion, tomatoes, or carrots.

1 pound spinach leaves
4 cups vegetable broth
2 tablespoons butter
½ onion, chopped
1 tablespoon all-purpose flour
Salt and pepper
Dash of grated nutmeg
½ cup evaporated milk (or half and half)
Greek yogurt or sour cream

You can make croutons with both fresh or stale bread to sprinkle on this soup. Cut the bread into ½-inch squares, drizzle with olive oil and a few thyme leaves, and bake in the oven at 300°F until golden and crunchy (about 20 minutes). Once the croutons are cold, you can store them in an airtight container for up to 4 days.

1. In a saucepan over medium heat, blanch the spinach in the vegetable broth until wilted. Turn off the heat and process in a blender or using an immersion blender, until creamy.
2. Melt the butter in the same saucepan over medium heat, and sauté the onion for 5 minutes, stirring occasionally. Add the flour, stirring constantly for 3 minutes. Make sure no lumps are formed.
3. Add the blended spinach, salt, and pepper, and keep stirring for 1 more minute.
4. Cook for 15 minutes, check the seasoning, and add evaporated milk. Turn the heat off.
5. Stir, and serve immediately with a dollop of yogurt or sour cream.

CHICKEN AGUADITO

Serves 4

Peruvians jokingly say this dish is a *levanta-muertos* (literally, that it wakes up the dead). It's usually eaten at dawn, after partying all night long, for its restoring and soothing qualities. The same soup made with duck is even more popular than this homey chicken version.

4 chicken thighs and legs
Salt and pepper
¼ cup vegetable oil
½ cup onion, finely chopped
2 garlic cloves, mashed
3 tablespoons *ají amarillo* paste
2 cups cilantro leaves (discard the stems)
4 cups chicken stock
1 cup beer (optional)
½ red bell pepper, diced
1 cup carrot, diced
1 cup corn kernels
½ cup white rice
4 small potatoes, peeled
½ cup green peas

1. Season the chicken with salt and pepper. Heat the vegetable oil in a saucepan over medium heat, and sear the chicken pieces. Transfer them to a plate, and sauté the onion, garlic, and *ají amarillo* paste in the same saucepan, until golden.
2. Process the cilantro leaves in a blender with ¼ cup water, until smooth. Add to the onion mixture, along with the chicken stock, beer, chicken, corn, and carrots. Bring to a boil, turn the heat to low, cover, and simmer for 30 minutes.
3. Add the rice and potatoes, put the lid on again, and simmer until the potatoes are tender and the rice is cooked. If the soup is too thick, add more stock. Taste for seasoning, and serve.

This dish is quite big, so I recommend you make it your only course. Even if you serve it in small bowls, the corn, potatoes, and rice will make it very filling.

MENESTRÓN

Serves 4

When Italians came to Peru many years ago, they brought with them their traditional dishes. These were quickly adopted by local cooks, who created Peruvianized versions of many of them, including the classic minestrone, which became the homey *menestrón*.

4 cups beef, chicken, or vegetable broth, or water
1 cup celery, chopped
1 cup onion or leek, chopped
4 garlic cloves, chopped
1 cup carrot, chopped
1 cup turnip, chopped
1 cup green beans
1 cup baby lima beans
1 cup potato, peeled and chopped
1 cup yucca, peeled and chopped
1 cup cabbage, coarsely shredded
1 cup giant kernel corn, or regular white corn
½ cup fresh white cheese, in cubes
Salt and pepper
1 cup small pasta, like penne or rigatoni

For the sauce:
½ onion, chopped
2 garlic cloves, chopped
2 tablespoons oil
1 cup basil leaves
1 cup spinach
Salt and pepper

1. In a saucepan over medium heat, cook the celery, onion or leek, garlic, carrot, turnip, green beans, lima beans, potato, yucca, cabbage, and corn, with water or stock to cover. When everything is tender, (about 35 minutes), season with salt and pepper. It will be very tasty. If you want to add some herbs while cooking, feel free to do so—parsley, bay leaf, or cilantro are some flavorful additions.
2. Add the pasta and cook for a few minutes longer, according to the package instructions.
3. To make the sauce, heat the oil in a pan over medium heat. Add onion and garlic, and cook, stirring for 5 minutes. Add the basil and spinach, stir until wilted, and season with salt and pepper. Transfer to a blender and process until smooth. Pour into the soup.
4. Cook the soup for another 5 minutes, just to heat it through, and serve.

There is nothing like a home made stock to enhance the flavor of this soup. Make yours when you have enough vegetables and or chicken bones in the fridge. Strain, cool, and freeze in ice cube trays. Transfer to freezer bags and keep frozen until needed.

SOPA CRIOLLA—BEEF AND ANGEL HAIR SOUP

Serves 4

The people of Lima love this soup, which can be made in less than 30 minutes. It is a nourishing and comforting soup that sticks to your ribs. The addition of angel hair pasta and the toasted bread on top make it a robust meal.

3 tablespoons vegetable oil
½ chopped onion
2 chopped garlic cloves
2 teaspoons *ají panca* paste
1 teaspoon dried oregano
2 tablespoons tomato paste
1 pound ground beef (or finely chopped meat)
4 cups beef stock, or water
4 ounces angel hair pasta
Salt and pepper
½ cup evaporated milk
4 slices white bread, toasted
4 fried eggs
4 parsley sprigs

If you don't want to use milk, you can simply leave it out of the recipe, to make this soup dairy free. You can also leave the egg out, or serve the soup with a poached egg instead.

1. Heat the oil in a saucepan over medium heat. Sauté the onion, garlic, and *ají panca*, stirring for 5 minutes. Add the oregano and tomato paste, stir, and add the ground meat. Cook until brown, and then add 4 cups boiling stock or water. Put the lid on, lower the heat, and simmer for 20 minutes.

2. Add the angel hair to the pan and cook for 3 minutes or until al dente. Season with salt and pepper. Turn off the heat and incorporate the milk.

3. Put a little oil in a skillet over medium heat, and fry the bread slices turning to brown both sides. Transfer to a plate covered with paper towels. Then fry the eggs, one by one, seasoning with salt.

4. Serve the soup in bowls, top with a toasted bread slice, and a fried egg on top of the bread. Garnish with a parsley sprig and serve.

CHUPE DE CAMARONES— HEARTY SHRIMP SOUP

Serves 6

Chupe de camarones is an empowering, and some say aphrodisiac, soup that is served in very large bowls. Peruvians have substantial appetites, but this meal satisfies them for the rest of the day.

½ cup *achiote* oil (see tip box)
1 onion, chopped
4 garlic cloves, chopped
1 tablespoon *ají panca* paste
1 tablespoon tomato paste
1 teaspoon dried oregano
6 cups shrimp or fish stock
½ cup white rice
1 pound potatoes, peeled (about 6 medium-sized potatoes)
2 ears of corn, broken into 3 pieces each
2 pounds shrimp, peeled and cleaned
1 cup green peas
1 cup *queso fresco*
1½ cups evaporated milk
Salt and pepper
⅓ cup vegetable oil
6 eggs
6 parsley sprigs to garnish

1. Heat the *achiote* oil in a saucepan over medium heat. Add the onion, garlic, and oregano, and sauté until golden. Add the tomato paste and continue cooking for 5 more minutes.
2. Add the shrimp or fish stock, and bring to a boil, skimming the stock every few minutes. Turn the heat to medium low, add the rice, and simmer partially covered for 15 minutes.
3. Add the potatoes and corn, and continue simmering until the potatoes are tender.
4. Add the peeled shrimp, and green peas, cook for 3 minutes.
5. Add the milk, salt, and pepper, and turn off the heat. Finally add the cheese.
6. Heat the vegetable oil in a skillet and fry the eggs, one by one, sunny-side up.
7. Place a few shrimp, some rice, 1 potato, and a piece of corn in each bowl. Cover with the hot soup, and top with a fried egg.
8. Garnish with parsley, and serve immediately.

To make the *achiote* oil, heat ½ cup vegetable oil at very low heat, and add 2 tablespoons *achiote* seeds. When the oil turns red, turn the heat off, let cool, and drain to discard the seeds. You can buy *achiote* in any Latin American grocery store.

RICE

ARROZ AL OLIVAR— BLACK OLIVE RICE

Serves 4

Peruvians love rice and black olives with similar intensity, and this dish combines both. You can serve it as a side dish, or make it a complete meal by serving it with shrimp. If you are a vegetarian, grate some Parmesan cheese on top to complement the intense olive flavor.

8 ounces pitted Alfonso olives
3 tablespoons vegetable oil
2 garlic cloves, chopped
2 cups white rice
½ cup raisins
1 red bell pepper, diced
Salt and pepper
½ cup pecans, finely chopped
½ cup Parmesan cheese (optional)
Parsley leaves, to garnish (optional)

Alfonso olives are similar to the Botija variety used in Peru, so use these if you can't find the latter. Other black olives will change the flavor. If buying them in a jar, drain well and rinse in cold water as they may be too salty.

1. Puree the olives in a blender or a food processor. Reserve.
2. Fry the garlic for a minute or two in oil over medium heat. Do not let it brown.
3. Add the olive paste, rice, raisins, red bell pepper, salt, and black pepper, mixing well. Be careful when adding salt because the olives are salty.
4. Pour 3 cups boiling water into the rice. Bring to a boil, lower the heat to low, cover, and cook until the rice is tender. Stir with a fork, cover again, turn off the heat, and let rest for a few minutes.
5. Serve the rice sprinkled with pecans, Parmesan cheese, and parsley.

RISOTTO WITH AJÍ AMARILLO SAUCE AND SIRLOIN MEDALLIONS

Serves 4

The secrets for a good risotto are: (a) using short grain rice, like Arborio; (b) not washing the rice before using, so you don't throw away the starch that gives it its delicious creaminess; (c) stirring the rice and adding hot stock continuously, until it has the desired al dente texture.

¼ cup olive oil, plus 2 tablespoons
½ cup white onion, finely chopped
1 garlic clove, finely chopped
½–1 cup fresh *ají amarillo* paste (if using jarred *ají* paste, sample it first so you won't ruin the risotto with very hot *ají*)
2 cups Arborio rice
1 cup white wine
5 cups hot vegetable stock
Salt and pepper
1 cup *queso fresco*, diced (or feta)
2 tablespoons parsley and/or chives, chopped
4 sirloin medallions
Parmesan cheese, grated

You can substitute *ají amarillo* paste with *salsa Huancaína*. This is a creative and mouth-watering way to use any leftover cream when you make *papa a la Huancaína*.

1. In a heavy saucepan, heat ½ cup oil over medium heat, add the onion and garlic, lower the heat, and cook until the onion looks very soft. Add the *ají amarillo* and continue cooking for 5 more minutes.
2. Add the rice, stir, turn the heat back to medium, and cook for about 5 minutes.
3. Add the white wine to the rice, stir, and bring to a boil, cooking until the liquid evaporates. Season with salt and pepper.
4. Start adding the hot vegetable stock, a ladle at a time, stirring frequently until the rice is al dente and looks creamy. Stop adding stock to the rice once it's done because it will turn mushy.
5. Turn the heat to very low. Add the diced *queso fresco* and herbs.
6. Add 2 extra tablespoons olive oil and stir.
7. When the risotto is almost ready (or earlier if you want the meat well done), season the sirloin medallions with salt and pepper. Cook to your taste.
8. Put a sirloin medallion on top of each risotto plate, and serve immediately, sprinkled with Parmesan cheese.

RICE WITH SCALLOPS

Serves 4

Peru is a country that prides itself on the quality of its fish and seafood, and it has every reason to do so. The cold Humboldt current that flows along our coasts creates excellent quality plankton, (this is the food that seafood eat), so our sea critters are very well nourished. Despite this logical explanation, we love to romanticize things and say the reason behind this good fortune is that God was born in our land.

3 cups white rice, cooked
4 tablespoons vegetable oil
1 cup red onion, chopped
2 garlic cloves, chopped
2 tablespoons *ají amarillo* paste
1 cup white corn kernels
1 cup carrot, diced
1 cup green peas
1 cup red bell pepper, diced
½ cup white wine
Salt and pepper
½ cup vegetable or fish stock
3 cups white rice, cooked
1 pound scallops (with or without the roe)
2 tablespoons chopped cilantro
Lime slices

1. Heat the oil in a saucepan over medium heat. Add and sauté the onion and garlic in oil over medium heat, until translucent. Add *ají amarillo* paste, stirring well.
2. Add the corn, carrots, green peas, red bell pepper, white wine, stock, salt, and pepper. Cook for a few minutes, until the vegetables are tender. Add the rice and cilantro. Stir.
3. Finally add the scallops, stir, and cover the pan. Turn off the heat and let everything steam for 5 minutes.
4. Sprinkle with cilantro and serve with lime slices on the side.

When you buy fresh scallops in Peru, they usually come with their bright orange/red roe still attached to them, and this gives them an extra intensity. Health-conscious eaters, however, try to avoid eating this, as it is believed to be very high in cholesterol.

RICE WITH SEAFOOD

Serves 2

This dish is every Peruvian´s dream come true, as it puts together two of our great culinary loves: seafood and rice. Every time I make it, my mind wanders back to a beautiful restaurant in Lima called Costa Verde, overlooking the Pacific Ocean and the majestic cliffs that make our city as unique as its food.

8 ounces raw seafood
  (calamari rings, peeled shrimp,
  clams, scallops, etc.)
2 cups cooked white rice
3 tablespoons vegetable oil
½ cup red onion, finely diced
3 garlic cloves, diced
1–2 tablespoons *ají amarillo*,
  chopped
1 tomato, peeled, seeded, and
  chopped (or 1 tablespoon tomato
  paste)
½ teaspoon dried oregano
1 bay leaf
¼ cup *achiote* oil (see tip box)
¼ cup white wine
¼ cup fish stock
½ cup roasted red bell pepper
½ cup green peas
½ cup grated Parmesan cheese
1 tablespoon cilantro leaves,
  chopped
Salt and pepper

1. Heat the oil in a saucepan over high heat and cook the onion, stirring for 3 minutes.
2. Lower the heat to medium, add the garlic, and continue cooking for 2 more minutes.
3. Add the chopped tomato (or tomato paste), *ají amarillo*, dried oregano, bay leaf, and *achiote* oil. Cook for 5 minutes.
4. Add the white wine, bring to a boil, and when it has almost completely evaporared, add the fish stock, rice, and seafood. Cook, stirring for 5 minutes. Discard the bay leaf.
5. Incorporate the bell pepper, green peas, Parmesan cheese, cilantro leaves, salt, and pepper.
6. Serve immediately.

To make *achiote* oil, put ½ cup vegetable oil in a small saucepan, with 1 tablespoon *achiote* seeds. Heat over a very low flame until the oil turns red. Once cool, drain and discard the seeds. Pour the oil in a jar and use as needed (you can add it to any recipe to give it a red color).

ARROZ CON PATO— RICE WITH DUCK

Serves 4

Peruvian native ducks have been enjoyed in many different preparations for centuries, but the combination of rice with cilantro paste and vegetables is perhaps the most popular of them all. This northern dish is usually prepared with grated *loche* squash to add even more flavor and creaminess.

4 duck legs (with thighs)
2 cups beer, plus 1 cup
½ cup vegetable oil, divided
1 red onion, chopped
2 garlic cloves, chopped
3 tablespoons *ají amarillo* paste
Salt and pepper
1 teaspoon ground cumin
½ teaspoon ground turmeric
**2 cups cilantro leaves processed
    with ½ cup water**
½ cup carrot, diced
3 cups rice
**1 red bell pepper, roasted and
    sliced**
1 cup green peas
***Salsa criolla* (p. 79)**

You may use duck breasts if you want, but remember that these have a shorter cooking time and should be taken out of the pan sooner.

1. Combine duck legs and 2 cups beer in a bowl or glass baking pan. Cover and refrigerate for up to 12 hours. Drain and dry with paper towels.
2. Heat ¼ cup oil in a saucepan over medium heat and sear the duck legs until golden. Transfer to a plate and keep covered. In the same saucepan sauté the onion, garlic, and *ají amarillo* paste for 10 minutes. Add salt, pepper, cumin, turmeric, and cilantro paste. Cook for 5 minutes longer.
3. Put the duck legs back in the saucepan; add the remaining beer and 4 cups of water. Bring to a boil, cover tightly with a lid, turn the heat to low, and simmer for 1½ hours until the duck legs are very tender. Add the carrots for the last 15 minutes of cooking.
4. In another saucepan, heat the remaining oil over medium heat, add the rice, and stir until well coated with the oil.
5. Add 4½ cups of the hot stock in which the duck legs cooked. Put the lid on, lower the heat, and cook for 10 minutes. Add the green peas and the diced bell pepper, stir with a fork, and cook for 10 more minutes.
6. Taste to see if it's done, and add a little hot stock if you need to cook it for a bit longer.
7. Turn off the heat. To serve put a portion of rice on each plate and top with the duck meat. Serve with *salsa criolla* on the side.

VEGETARIAN ARROZ CON POLLO

Makes 4

Rice in Peru is the most popular side dish along with potatoes, but it is also a beloved entrée. *Arroz con pollo*, or rice with chicken, is one of our all-time favorite rice dishes. You can enjoy it freshly made or after a day in the fridge; with or without chicken; and with *salsa criolla, Huancaina* sauce, or a fried egg on top.

2 bunches cilantro (only the leaves)
4 spinach leaves
2 tablespoons vegetable oil
1 cup red onion, chopped
3 garlic cloves, chopped
3 tablespoons *ají amarillo* **paste**
2 cups vegetable stock
2 cups beer (optional)
2 cups white rice
Salt and pepper
¼ cup carrots, diced
1 red bell pepper, cut in slices
1 cup white corn
1 cup green peas
Salsa criolla **(p. 79)**

1. Process the cilantro and spinach in a blender with ½ cup water. Reserve.
2. Heat 2 tablespoons vegetable oil in a saucepan over medium heat. Sauté the onion, garlic, and *ají amarillo*, stirring for 5 minutes. Add the cilantro mixture and fry for 3 minutes.
3. Add the rice, stirring for a couple minutes, and then pour in the vegetable stock, beer, carrots, red bell pepper, and corn. Season with salt and pepper, and stir well. (If you don't use beer, add more vegetable stock).
4. Bring to a boil, put the lid on, lower the heat, and cook undisturbed for about 20 minutes or until the rice is cooked.
5. Add the peas, stir with a kitchen fork, put the lid back on, and cook for an extra 5 minutes.
6. Serve the rice topped with *salsa criolla*.

To make the original version with chicken, use any part of the chicken, and sear with oil until golden. Transfer to a plate and cover. Follow steps 1 and 2 using the same pan where you seared the chicken. Add the chicken, stock, and beer to the pan, and cook, covered, for 30 minutes. Only then go to step 3.

RISOTTO WITH LOMO SALTADO

Serves 3

This dish is a modern fusion created by Italian-Peruvian cooks, to bring their favorite preparations together in one meal.

Lomo saltado **(p. 137), without rice nor French fries**
⅓ cup olive oil
½ onion, finely chopped
2 garlic cloves, finely chopped
1 cup Arborio rice
1 cup white wine
4 cups hot vegetable stock
Salt and pepper
2 tablespoons butter

Change the flavor of this tasty risotto using chicken or shrimp instead of beef. If you want the *lomo saltado* to be juicier add ½ cup beef stock along with the soy sauce.

1. Heat the oil in a saucepan over medium heat. Add onion and garlic and cook, stirring occasionally until translucent.
2. Add the rice and continue stirring for 7 minutes.
3. Add the white wine, bring to a boil, and when it evaporates, start adding ladlefuls of the simmering stock. Stir the rice as you do this, until the stock is absorbed and the rice is al dente. Season with salt and pepper during this process.
4. Finally, add the butter and stir until it melts.
5. When your risotto is almost ready, make the *lomo saltado*.
6. Serve a portion of risotto on each plate and top it with *lomo saltado*.
7. Serve at once.

ARROZ CHAUFA— FISH STIR-FRIED RICE

Serves 3

We love *arroz chaufa*, the famous stir-fried rice from Chinese descent, which Peruvians adopted as ours many decades ago. Addicted to its delectable simplicitiy, we make it at home with leftover rice, and any meat or vegetable lingering in the fridge.

1 pound fish fillets
4 tablespoons soy sauce, divided
4 tablespoons vegetable oil, divided
2 eggs, lightly beaten
2 garlic cloves, chopped
2 teaspoons grated ginger
½ cup snow peas, sliced
2 cups cold, unsalted cooked white rice
¼ cup red bell pepper, thinly sliced
½ cup green peas, cooked
½ cup soy sprouts
1 teaspoon sesame oil
2 scallions, white and green parts sliced
2 tablespoons toasted sesame seeds (optional)

This recipe is very flexible. There are versions made with pork, chicken, seafood, or veggies, while others are made only with rice, eggs, garlic, ginger, and soy sauce. The latter may be simple, but it is equally flavorful.

1. Cut the fish fillets in bite-size pieces and season with one tablespoon soy sauce.
2. Heat one tablespoon vegetable oil in a wok or pan over medium heat, and add the eggs to make a thin omelette. After a couple of minutes, turn the omelette and cook just a few seconds on the other side. Transfer to a cutting board and cut in thin slices. Reserve.
3. In the same wok, heat the remaining oil and stir-fry the fish, stirring carefully until golden but do not overcook. Transfer to a plate and reserve.
4. In the same wok, add the garlic, ginger, snow peas, red bell pepper, and cold rice, and stir-fry until hot. Add the green peas and soy sprouts.
5. Season with the remaining soy sauce and one teaspoon sesame oil. Turn off the heat and sprinkle everything with chopped scallions and sesame seeds. Serve immediately.

LIMA BEAN TACU TACU

Serves 4

Tacu tacu is a traditional dish that is hearty enough to satisfy not only a craving but a good appetite. Usually made with leftover canary beans, it is also commonly prepared with any other kind of legumes, such as lentils, garbanzos, black beans, or split peas.

½ cup vegetable oil, divided
½ cup scallions or red onion, chopped
2 garlic cloves, chopped
2 tablespoons *ají amarillo* paste (optional)
3 cups leftover cooked dried lima beans
1½ cup leftover cooked white rice
8 ripe mini bananas
4 eggs
Salt and pepper
2 cups *salsa criolla* (p. 79)
4 cilantro sprigs

In my kitchen, *tacu tacu* is always made vegetarian, as I don´t use hamhock or any other meat in the cooking of the beans, (most households and restaurants do).

1. Heat 2 tablespoons vegetable oil in a skillet over medium heat. Add the scallions or onion, garlic, and *ají amarillo* paste, and cook until everything is very soft.
2. Add the lima beans, stirring frequently with a wooden spoon and pressing to mash them. Add the rice. Continue to cook until the mixture looks like a thick puree.
3. Heat 1 tablespoon oil in a small frying pan over medium heat. When hot, add about ½ or ¾ cup of the lima bean and rice mixture, giving it the shape of a hamburger, and fry until a golden crust is formed. Using a plate, turn it upside down and return to the pan to fry it on the other side.
4. Heat more oil in another frying pan. Peel the mini bananas and fry until golden. Then fry the eggs, one by one, seasoning with salt and pepper.
5. Serve the *tacu tacu* with a fried egg on top, and place two fried bananas on the side.
6. Garnish with *salsa criolla* and a few cilantro sprigs, and serve immediately.

ENTRÉES

LOCRO

Makes 4

Locro is the ultimate vegetarian dish of the Andes. To make it we use a squash called *macre*, but if you´re not in Peru, feel free to experiment with any pumpkin available. If you do this, don't forget to adjust the cooking time. You should aim for a creamy texture.

¼ cup vegetable oil
1 red onion, chopped
3 garlic cloves, mashed
2 tablespoons *ají amarillo* paste
2 pounds *macre* squash
   (or butternut squash), peeled and
   diced
2 medium white potatoes, peeled
   and diced
1 cup giant kernel corn (or any
   white corn)
2 cups vegetable stock
Salt and pepper
½ cup green peas
½ cup unsweetened evaporated
   milk
1 cup *queso fresco* (or feta), diced
2 tablespoons cilantro leaves,
   chopped
2 tablespoons parsley leaves,
   chopped
2 cups cooked white rice (optional)

1. Heat the vegetable oil in a saucepan over medium heat. Add the onion and garlic, and sauté until translucent.
2. Add the squash, potatoes, corn, vegetable stock, salt, and pepper. Lower the heat and simmer, semi covered, stirring occasionally until the vegetables are tender.
3. Finally add the green peas, evaporated milk, and *queso fresco*. Stir quickly and turn off the heat.
4. Taste for seasoning, add the herbs, stir, and serve with white rice on the side.

Locro leftovers can be used to make an original *tacu tacu*, by mixing them with leftover rice, and frying them shaped into patties.

TALLARINES VERDES

Serves 4

Pesto was first brought to Peru by Italian immigrants from Liguria, which is known to be the cradle of this popular sauce, and boasts of having the most aromatic basil in the world. Their simple yet exquisite gastronomy had a permanent influence on Peruvian cuisine; and the original *pesto ligure* became the popular *tallarines verdes* (green noodles).

¼ **cup olive oil**
¼ **cup red onion, diced**
2 **garlic cloves, chopped**
4 **cups spinach leaves**
1 **cup basil leaves**
¾ **cup evaporated milk**
½ **cup *queso fresco* (or feta)**
¼ **cup pecans**
Salt and pepper
1 **pound spaghetti**
1 **cup cooked green beans**
½ **cup Parmesan cheese, grated**

1. Heat the oil in a skillet over medium heat. Sauté the onion until transparent, stirring occasionally (about 5 minutes). Turn off the heat and reserve.
2. Pour boiling water over the spinach and basil leaves. Drain.
3. Process the onion, and its oil, garlic, spinach, basil, evaporated milk, *queso fresco*, pecans, salt, and pepper in a blender until smooth.
4. Cook the pasta in salted boiling water following the package instructions.
5. Drain the pasta and mix with the spinach-basil cream, and top it with green beans and grated Parmesan cheese.

Want to raise the health bar on this dish? Try mixing in some steamed or slightly sautéed zucchini slices, asparagus, fava beans, and peas. For a vegan rendition, substitute the milk with unsweetened soy, almond, or pecan milk, and the cheese with tofu or cashew cheese.

SALCHIPAPAS

Serves 2

This Peruvian fast-food dish is exactly what its name indicates: sausages (*salchichas*), and potatoes (*papas*). With such a short list of ingredients, you hardly need a recipe at all.

½ cup vegetable oil for frying, plus
   1 tablespoon
1 Russet potato, peeled and cut in
   sticks
Salt and pepper
4 sausages
4 eggs (optional)
Ketchup
Mustard
Ají amarillo paste
Mayonnaise
2 parsley leaves, to garnish

Some variations of *salchipapas* include different kinds of sausages, and sweet potatoes or yucca fries instead of potato fries.

1. Heat ½ cup vegetable oil in a heavy saucepan over high heat.
2. Dry the potatoes with paper towels and fry until golden brown. If you are using the frozen ready-made variety, heat them in a 450°F oven for 18 minutes.
3. Once they're done, season the fries with salt.
4. Cut the sausages in ¼-inch round slices. Heat a tablespoon oil in a skillet. Sauté the sausages until golden.
5. Combine the sausages and fries on two plates.
6. Fry the eggs, sunny side up, (if using) and place two on top of the sausage mixture. Garnish with parsley leaves.
7. Serve with ketchup, mustard, *ají amarillo* paste, and mayonnaise on the side.

LOMO A LO POBRE

Serves 4

This poor man´s steak recipe may use humble ingredients, but the amount of food it requires to be made, and its intense flavors, are anything but poor. A hearty *tacu tacu* (rice and beans) is covered with a breaded steak, fried eggs, and topped with *salsa criolla*. You will never be hungry when this dish is around.

3 tablespoons + ½ cup vegetable oil
⅓ cup red onion, finely chopped
2 garlic cloves, finely chopped
1 tablespoon *ají amarillo* paste (or to taste)
½ teaspoon dried oregano
2 cups leftover canary beans, cooked
Salt and pepper
2 cups leftover white rice, cooked
4 small ripe mini bananas, peeled
4 steaks
1 cup flour
10 eggs, (separate 2 of them and beat them slightly)
1 cup breadcrumbs
***Salsa criolla* (p. 79)**

Tacu *tacu* is a simple dish that can be served on its own, or topped with *salsa criolla*. You can also crown it with fried eggs.

1. Heat 2 tablespoons of oil in a pan and cook the onion and garlic, stirring frequently. Add the *ají amarillo* paste and oregano.
2. Add and stir the beans, mashing them with a wooden spoon, or even better, with a potato masher. Season with salt and pepper.
3. Add the rice and continue stirring and mashing until the mixture is thick like a paste.
4. Divide in four portions. Fry each portion individually, giving it a football shape by moving the pan back and forth with a firm but light movement. If this doesn't work out, fry them like you would a hamburger. The outer layer of the *tacu tacu* must be slightly crispy while the inside should remain mushy.
5. Fry the bananas in 1 tablespoon of hot oil, until golden, and reserve.
6. In the meantime, prepare the steaks. First, season them with salt and pepper.
7. Put the flour in one bowl, the beaten eggs in a second bowl, and the breadcrumbs in a third one.
8. Dip each steak in flour, then in the beaten eggs, and finally in the breadcrumbs, shaking any excess.
9. Heat the remaining oil in a frying pan over medium heat. Fry the steaks until golden brown on both sides.
10. In another skillet, fry the eggs sunny-side up.
11. Put a portion of *tacu tacu* on each plate. Top with a breaded steak, and top this with two fried eggs. Serve a fried banana next to it, and *salsa criolla* on the side.

LOMO SALTADO

Serves 2

This robust entrée is the result of the fusion between Peruvian and Chinese cuisines. If you feel like making it, make sure you have everything ready to throw in the pan, because it cooks rather quickly. Dinner will be ready in just a few minutes.

1 pound sirloin steak, cut in bite-size pieces
2 garlic cloves, finely diced
3 tablespoons vegetable oil
1 red onion, thickly sliced
2 tomatoes, cut in thick slices
1 *ají amarillo*, cut in thin slices (or use 1 tablespoon *ají amarillo* paste)
4 tablespoons red wine vinegar
4 tablespoons soy sauce
Salt and pepper
½ cup fresh cilantro, chopped
2 cups French fries
1½ cups cooked white rice

1. Season the steak with salt, pepper, and garlic.
2. Put a wok or a skillet over high heat. When very hot, add the oil and then meat, a few slices at a time so they turn golden brown instead of steaming. Transfer the cooked pieces to a bowl before adding more raw pieces to the wok. Repeat with all the steak.
3. Add all the cooked steak pieces, onion, tomato, and *ají amarillo* to the same wok, stirring for a couple of minutes.
4. Add the vinegar and soy sauce down the sides of the pan, and combine everything. Season to taste with salt and pepper.
5. Turn off the heat, add the chopped cilantro, and serve at once with French fries and white rice.

Instead of sirloin steak, I often use chicken, veggies (wonderful with portobello mushrooms cut in strips to substitute the meat), or shrimp. Nowadays chefs like making fashionable versions with spaghetti instead of rice and fries, or using the stir-fry as an empanada or *tequeño* filling.

LOMO A LO MACHO

Serves 4

The fiery hot seafood sauce known as *a lo macho* is usually served over fish, but here you have a nontraditional variation using beef as the main ingredient.

4 sirloin medallions
Salt and pepper
½ cup vegetable oil
1 cup red onion, chopped
4 garlic cloves, chopped
1 teaspoon paprika
½ teaspoon dried oregano
½ cup *ají amarillo* paste
2 tomatoes, peeled, seeded, and chopped
½ cup white wine
2 cups fish stock
2 tablespoons potato starch
8 mussels
4 ounces scallops, cleaned
4 ounces shrimp, peeled and deveined
4 ounces cooked squid, cut into rings
1 tablespoon cilantro, chopped
½ cup microgreens for garnish (optional)

1. Season the sirloin with salt and pepper. Heat 2 tablespoons of oil in a skillet over medium heat, add the steaks, and sear on both sides until golden.
2. In the meantime, heat the rest of the oil in a skillet over medium heat. Add the onions, garlic, paprika, and oregano, and sauté for 5 minutes or until the onion looks translucent. Add the *ají amarillo* paste, cook stirring for 3 minutes, and add the tomatoes, cooking for 5 more minutes. Pour the wine, bring to a boil, lower the heat, and simmer for 3 minutes. Season with salt and pepper.
3. Add the fish stock and simmer for 10 minutes. Dissolve the potato starch in 3 tablespoons cold water, add to the saucepan, a little at a time, and stir until everything is slightly thick. Finally add the seafood, stir, and sprinkle with cilantro, salt, and pepper. Turn off the heat.
4. Transfer the sirloin medallions to 4 plates, surround with the seafood sauce, garnish the steaks with microgreens, and serve.

Serve this dish with potatoes that have been boiled, thickly sliced, and fried in a skillet with a little olive oil until golden brown.

SECO DE CARNE

Serves 4

Antonella Delfino shared this scrumptious recipe with us. This cilantro stew is traditionally made with goat in the north of Peru, and it is usually served with white fluffy rice, mashed canary or lima beans, and some olive oil drizzled on top.

3 cups cilantro leaves
2 cups spinach
½ cup vegetable oil
2 pounds boneless chuck roast, cut in 2 × 2–inch pieces
1 chopped red onion
2 chopped garlic cloves
1 tablespoon *ají amarillo* paste
2 potatoes, cut in four pieces
Salt and pepper
¾ cup green peas
¾ cup diced carrots
Cooked white rice (optional)
Cooked canary beans (optional)

If you have fresh cilantro in the fridge and do not know what to do with it, blend it with a little bit of water to form a paste, and put it in the freezer. This way, you will have cilantro paste ready to use in many soups and stews. Peruvians use only the leaves, but you can include the stems and even the roots to add another layer of flavor to some dishes.

1. Put the cilantro and spinach in a blender and process with one cup water. Reserve.
2. Heat the oil in a saucepan over high heat, and when it is very hot, sear the beef pieces until they are golden brown.
3. Add the onions, garlic, and *ají amarillo* paste, and cook until the onions are soft and translucent, stirring occasionally.
4. Pour the cilantro mix and turn up to medium heat. Stir constantly until the water evaporates. The cilantro mixture is going to become a dark green color.
5. Pour 6 cups of water and simmer over low heat for 2 hours with the lid on. Check constantly and add more water if necessary. Season with salt and pepper.
6. When the meat is fork tender, add the potatoes, green peas and carrots. Cook uncovered for 15 minutes or until the vegetables are tender.
7. The stew is ready when the veggies are cooked and the sauce is slightly thick. Taste for seasoning.
8. Serve with white rice and mashed canary beans.

GNOCCHI WITH SECO SAUCE

Makes 4

The easiest way to turn any dish vegetarian is by replacing the meat with a vegetarian protein such as tofu, soy meat, or portobello mushrooms. In this recipe, however, we did something completely new: we turned the potatoes that usually accompany this traditional entrée into gnocchi, and left the meat completely out of the formula.

3 tablespoons vegetable oil
1 medium red onion, chopped
4 garlic cloves, chopped
1 tablespoon *ají amarillo* paste (optional)
2 tomatoes, peeled, seeded, and chopped
½ red bell pepper, diced
¾ cup cilantro leaves, blended with ¼ cup water
1 cup vegetable stock
Salt and pepper
1 cup fava beans or green peas, cooked
1 pound potato gnocchi
Parmesan cheese

1. Heat the vegetable oil in a saucepan over medium heat. Add the onion and garlic, and cook, stirring until very tender (about 5–7 minutes).
2. Add the *ají amarillo* paste, tomatoes, red bell pepper, cilantro paste, salt, and pepper.
3. Cook for 5 minutes, stirring occasionally.
4. Add the vegetable stock, put the lid on, lower the heat to low, and simmer for 15 minutes. Add the cooked fava beans or green peas and keep warm. Put the lid on and turn the heat off.
5. In the meantime, cook the gnocchi in boiling salted water. They are ready when they float.
6. Drain and combine with the sauce.
7. Serve sprinkled with Parmesan cheese.

If you wish, you can add more vegetables and diced potatoes on top of everything else; or use pasta or couscous instead of gnocchi.

ASADO—ROAST BEEF

Serves 6

This is a homey dish, usually served with rice and mashed potatoes on the side, and it's one more of Antonella Delfino's delicious family recipes. The type of meat used (eye round), needs to cook for a long time in a flavorful broth. You may want to marinate the beef overnight to infuse it with more taste, but that is only if you have the time to do it.

3 tablespoons vegetable oil
2 pounds eye round, fat removed
1 large red onion, cut in six pieces
3 tomatoes, cut in four pieces each
4 garlic cloves
5 dried mushrooms
¾ bottle red wine
4 cups water
⅓ cup soy sauce
2 tablespoons Worcestershire sauce
1½ tablespoons potato starch
   (*chuño*)
Salt and pepper
Cooked rice (optional)
Mashed potatoes (optional)

Like many other stews, *asado* is much better the day after it has been cooked. If you have the time, cook it in advance so the flavors meld. It is also a good dish to have ready when you have guests, because you only need to reheat it.

1. Heat the oil in a heavy saucepan over high heat, add the meat, and sear it until it forms a golden crust all over.
2. Add the onions, tomatoes, and garlic, and stir until they start to release their juices.
3. Meanwhile, cover the dried mushrooms for 30 minutes with one cup boiling water. Strain the liquid through a colander covered with paper towels (they are full of dirt, so you want to get rid of it). Squeeze the mushrooms, and cut in ½-inch slices. Reserve the liquid.
4. Add half the bottle of wine to the pan, along with the soy sauce, Worcestershire sauce, dried mushrooms with soaking water, and the remaining water. Season with salt and pepper.
5. Turn the heat to low, cover with a tight-fitting lid, and cook undisturbed for an hour.
6. Take the beef out of the saucepan, drain well, put on a chopping board, and thinly slice it into ¼-inch pieces. An electric knife is very helpful for this, but a sharp knife is fine.
7. Strain the vegetables and put the cooking liquid back in the saucepan. Add the remaining wine and more water if necessary.
8. Put the slices of meat back in the saucepan, and season with salt, pepper, and more soy sauce, to taste.
9. Continue cooking over low heat until the meat is fork tender (about 1 more hour).
10. When the meat is ready, dissolve the potato starch in 3 tablespoons water and gradually add it to the saucepan, stirring constantly with a wooden spoon until the sauce becomes thick enough to lightly cover the spoon.
11. Serve with rice and/or mashed potatoes on the side.

PASTEL DE CHOCLO— CORN PUDDING

Serves 8

Corn is one of those ingredients you could use over and over in countless preparations, either savory or sweet, and never get tired of it. In Peru for instance, we have innumerable ways of using this ingredient, but one of the most popular, without a doubt, is our beloved corn pudding, or pastel de choclo, filled with beef, raisins, black olives, and hard-boiled eggs.

⅓ **cup vegetable oil, divided**
1 **pound ground beef**
2 **medium red onions, finely chopped**
2 **garlic cloves, finely chopped**
1 **tablespoon tomato paste**
½ **cup beef stock**
½ **cup raisins**
3 **hard-boiled eggs, coarsely chopped**
½ **cup sliced black olives**
4 **cups fresh white corn kernels**
½ **cup half and half**
¾ **cup unsalted butter, melted**
5 **tablespoons sugar**
Salt and pepper
5 **eggs, whites and yolks separated**
1 **egg yolk combined with 2 tablespoons water**
¼ **teaspoon aniseed**

Make it vegetarian using slices of queso fresco or feta, and sliced black olives as the filling.

1. Heat ¼ cup oil in a skillet over high heat. Add the ground beef and cook for 10 minutes stirring constantly. Transfer to a bowl. In the same skillet heat the remaining oil, add onion and garlic, and cook stirring a few times until transparent. Add tomato paste, and beef stock or water, cook for 5 minutes, and return the meat to the pan. It should be saucy.

2. Incorporate raisins, hard-boiled eggs, and olives. Stir and turn off the heat. Reserve.

3. Preheat the oven to 350°F. In a blender process the corn kernels with milk and melted butter. Add sugar, salt, pepper, and egg yolks. Transfer to a bowl, and stir with a wooden spoon until the mixture looks very soft. Beat the egg whites until firm, and fold into the corn mixture.

4. Have a rectangular baking pan ready. Pour half the corn mixture in the pan, cover with the cooked beef and top with the remaining corn. Brush the surface of the corn with the egg yolk and water mixture, sprinkle with aniseed, and bake for 45 minutes or until golden brown and firm.

5. Serve with *ají amarillo* sauce, *Huancaina* sauce, or *salsa criolla*.

AJÍ DE GALLINA

Serves 4

This dish is neither a stew nor a fricassee, but a flavorful sauce to which cooked chicken is added. There are three basic steps in the preparation: cooking the poultry, making the sauce, and combining both to meld the flavors. To complete the dish, serve boiled yellow potatoes and white fluffy rice on the same plate.

1 chicken breast
3 cups water
Salt and pepper
3 slices white bread
¼ cup vegetable oil
½ red onion, finely chopped
2 garlic cloves, finely chopped
2 tablespoons *ají amarillo* paste
½ teaspoon dried oregano
½ cup pecans, finely chopped
½ cup Parmesan cheese, grated
½ cup evaporated milk or half and half
Salt and pepper
2 medium potatoes, boiled, peeled, and sliced
4 Alfonso olives
3 cups cooked white rice
2 hard-boiled eggs
4 parsley sprigs for decoration (optional)

Some cooks make this recipe using fish or shrimp instead of chicken. There are even versions with canned tuna! You can use *ají de gallina* to fill empanadas, ravioli, lasagna, tartlets, and more.

1. Cook the chicken breast with water, salt, and pepper, in a heavy saucepan over medium heat (about 20 minutes). You can add a parsley sprig or a bay leaf if you want more flavor in your stock.
2. When the chicken is tender, take it out of the water and shred the meat with two forks or with your fingers. Strain the stock and reserve.
3. Put the bread in a bowl and add one cup of the reserved stock. When the bread has absorbed all the stock, process in a blender to form a loose paste. Reserve.
4. Heat the oil in the same saucepan over medium heat. Cook the onion and garlic for about 7 minutes. Stir frequently and don´t let them brown. When the onion is very soft and almost transparent, stir in the *ají amarillo* paste and dried oregano, and keep cooking for 5 more minutes.
5. Add the bread and one more cup of chicken stock to the pan, stirring for 3 more minutes or until the mixture starts to thicken.
6. Add the shredded chicken, pecans, and cheese. Season lightly with salt and pepper because the cheese is already salty.
7. Finally, incorporate the evaporated milk or half and half, stir, and turn off the heat. If it looks too thick, thin it with more chicken stock. The sauce should be creamy, covering every chicken strand.
8. Put 2 slices of potato on each plate. Cover with the chicken mixture and serve with white rice on the side.
9. Garnish with hard-boiled eggs cut in quarters, Alfonso olives, and a parsley sprig.

CHICKEN STEW

Serves 4

This recipe is versatile in that it can be enjoyed for lunch or dinner, served with rice or pasta, it can be quickly turned into a vegetarian entrée, or become an enticing sandwich in the blink of an eye. Change the vegetables to get a different dish every time (mushrooms and green beans are good choices). Replace the potatoes in the stew with a side of mashed potatoes, or if you are in a luxurious mood, a hearty potato gratin makes another wonderful side.

4 chicken legs and thighs
Salt and pepper
4 tablespoons vegetable oil
1 cup onion, finely diced
2 garlic cloves, finely diced
2 tablespoons tomato paste
½ cup sweet wine (optional)
2 cups chicken stock
1 bay leaf
4 medium-sized yellow potatoes, peeled
1 cup carrots, peeled and cut in thin slices
½ cup green peas
½ cup raisins
White fluffy rice or pasta
Parsley sprigs

If you are using also the breasts, keep in mind that these cook faster than the thighs. Take them out of the stew 20 minutes before it is ready so they don't overcook.

1. Season the chicken with salt and pepper.
2. Heat 2 tablespoons of oil in a saucepan over medium heat. Sear the chicken pieces until golden, turning once. Transfer to a bowl and reserve.
3. Add the remaining oil to the saucepan and when hot, add the onion and garlic. Cook at medium-high heat, stirring every few minutes, until soft, (about 7 minutes). Add the tomato paste and stir, cooking for 3 minutes.
4. Put the chicken back in the saucepan, add the wine, bring to a boil, and add the chicken stock and the bay leaf. Cover, lower the heat and cook for 30 minutes.
5. Add the potatoes, carrots, green peas, and raisins. Continue cooking for 15–20 minutes or until the vegetables are tender.
6. Serve with rice, or as a pasta sauce, and garnish with parsley sprigs.

POLLO AL SILLAO— CHICKEN WITH SOY SAUCE

Serves 6–8

When I find a recipe I love, I try as many variations of it as I can think of. Such is the case with this dish. Sometimes I use orange juice for the marinade; sometimes I only use butter and mustard. I have served it with potato gratin, sautéed vegetables, or stir-fried rice. You can try your own combinations, and pick the one you like the most.

8 chicken thighs with the skin on
4 garlic cloves, sliced or grated
1 lime (juice and zest)
1 tablespoon ginger, grated
½ cup soy sauce
½ cup honey
1 cup orange juice
2 tablespoons Dijon mustard
2 tablespoons melted butter
1½ tablespoons potato starch (*chuño*)

You may use chicken breasts, wings, or legs, adjusting the cooking time, to make this recipe.

Serve with white rice, stir-fried veggies, or sliced and roasted sweet potatoes.

1. Place the chicken in a baking pan. I left the skin on because it protects the flesh in the oven, but feel free to use skinned chicken if you prefer.
2. Season with garlic, lime juice and zest, and ginger.
3. Combine the soy sauce, honey, orange juice, mustard, and butter, in a small bowl. Pour this over the chicken. Cover and marinate overnight or at least for two hours, in the fridge.
4. Preheat the oven to 375°F.
5. Uncover the chicken and bake for 1 hour, basting every 20 minutes with its own juices. The chicken should have a beautiful brown color when it's ready.
6. Transfer the sauce to a small saucepan and put over medium heat. Dissolve the potato starch in 3 tablespoons of water, and add it to the saucepan, stirring constantly until slightly thick.
7. Serve the chicken with this sauce.

VEGETARIAN PICHUBERRY AND QUINOA CHILI

Serves 8

Even though this hearty soup is not Peruvian, we could say this version is a fusion, as it is filled with some of our favorite Peruvian superfoods. It is a creation of our friend and health maven, Manuel Villacorta.

½ **cup quinoa**
1 **cup water**
2 **tablespoons olive oil**
1 **yellow onion, chopped**
1 **small jalapeno, seeded and minced**
1 **cup diced carrot**
1 **cup diced celery**
1 **green bell pepper, seeded and chopped**
1 **large zucchini, cut in ½-inch cubes**
4 **cloves garlic, minced**
2 **cups pichuberries, (golden berries) halved**
1 **15-ounce can black beans with liquid**
1 **15-ounce can kidney beans with liquid**
1 **15-ounce can canary beans with liquid (or substitute pinto beans)**
1 **15-ounce can diced tomatoes**
1 **tablespoon ground cumin**
2 **tablespoons chili powder**
2 **teaspoons oregano**
1 **teaspoon smoked paprika (optional)**
Salt and pepper, to taste

Optional toppings:
Chopped scallions, avocado slices, sour cream or plain Greek yogurt, shredded cabbage or lettuce, tortilla strips, lime wedges, chopped pichuberries

1. In a saucepan over medium heat, bring 1 cup of water to a boil. Add the quinoa and lower the heat to a simmer. Cook covered until all the water is absorbed, (about 15–20 minutes). Fluff with a fork and set aside.
2. In a large saucepan, heat the olive oil over medium heat. Add the onion and cook until soft (about 5 minutes), stirring occasionally. Add the jalapeno, carrot, celery, bell pepper, zucchini, and garlic, and cook, stirring often, until the vegetables start to soften (about 10 minutes).
3. Stir in the pichuberries (or golden berries) and cook for another 3–5 minutes, until they start releasing some of their juices.
4. Add the cooked quinoa, beans along with their juices, canned tomatoes with juice, cumin, chili powder, oregano, smoked paprika, salt, and pepper. Stir to combine.
5. Cover the saucepan and let the chili simmer over low heat for 25–30 minutes, or until fragrant.
6. Serve warm, with your choice of toppings.

Chili is a hearty Tex-Mex bean soup that allows for hundreds of variations. This recipe adds quinoa and pichuberries for a healthy bonus and a Peruvian twist.

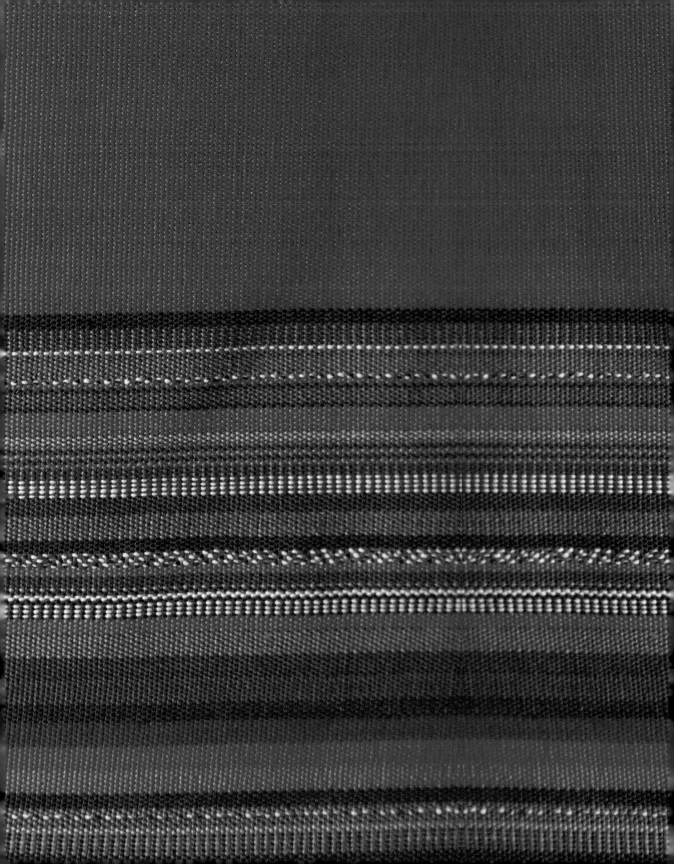

FROM THE SEA

SEAFOOD SALAD

Paola Cubas is the charming chef and owner of Pescatora, one of our favorite *cebiche* restaurants in Lima. She gave us this recipe a while back, and it became a big hit with our friends since day one, even though we have changed it a little bit. The best part of it is that it can be made in advance. Just make sure to add the avocado right before serving, so it doesn't turn brown.

12 ounces calamari, cut in ⅓-inch rings
8 ounces shrimp, cleaned
1 cup Peruvian giant corn kernels, cooked (or any white corn)
1 tomato, peeled and diced
4 Botija or Alfonso olives, sliced
2 tablespoons parsley, chopped
2 tablespoon basil leaves, sliced
1 teaspoon fresh thyme leaves, chopped
Salt and pepper
1 teaspoon garlic, mashed
½ cup olive oil
1 teaspoon Worcestershire sauce
1 tablespoon white wine vinegar
Juice of 3 limes
½ avocado, sliced
6 cherry tomatoes, cut in half
Basil leaves, to garnish

1. Clean the calamari under running water and cook in boiling salted water for 3 minutes. Drain and cool.
2. Cook the shrimp in boiling salted water for 3 minutes. Drain and cool.
3. Put the calamari and shrimp in a bowl with the corn kernels, tomato, olives, parsley, basil, and thyme.
4. Season with salt and pepper, garlic, olive oil, Worcestershire sauce, vinegar, and lime juice.
5. Serve on two plates and garnish with avocado slices, cherry tomatoes, and basil leaves.

If you want a spicy appetizer, add *ají amarillo* or *rocoto* paste to this salad, along with the lime juice.

FISH ESCABECHE

Serves 2

This cold fish dish is one of the most traditional on the coast of Peru. The secret is to make it the night before, giving the flavors and textures enough time to meld together and settle into their sweet spot.

2 halibut fillets
Salt and pepper
½ teaspoon ground cumin
½ cup flour
¼ cup olive oil
½ red onion, cut in thick slices or chunks
1 garlic clove, chopped
2 teaspoons *ají amarillo* paste
2 tablespoons vinegar
2 lettuce leaves
1 hard-boiled egg, sliced
4 *Botija* or Alfonso olives

Make *escabeche* with any white fish of your liking. Not in the mood for fish? No problem. You can make this recipe using chicken. For a vegetarian version use cooked lima beans or canary beans instead of fish.

1. Season the fish with salt, pepper, and cumin, and pass through the flour.
2. Heat half the olive oil in a frying pan over medium heat. Fry the fish on both sides, until golden (about 3–5 minutes). Reserve.
3. Bring water to a boil in a small saucepan, and blanch the onion for 1 minute. Drain.
4. Heat the rest of the oil in a small frying pan over medium heat. Sauté the garlic and chili paste for 2–3 minutes.
5. Add the onion, and vinegar, and season with salt and pepper. Simmer for about 5 minutes (add 2–4 tablespoons of water if it dries up).
6. Cover the fish with the onion mixture, put in a sealed container, and leave it in the fridge for as long as possible (overnight is best).
7. Serve cold over a lettuce leaf, and decorate with hard-boiled egg slices and black olives.

FISH FRITTERS

Serves 2

Depending on the quality of the fish you use, this rustic dish can turn into a real treat. We like using any white- fleshed fish, but feel free to improvise and choose whichever you like best. *Salsa criolla* is always the topping of choice, as well as tartar sauce and mayonnaise for the kids, or *ají amarillo* and *rocoto* sauces for the grownups.

**1 pound white fish fillets, cut in
   1-inch cubes
Salt and pepper
Juice of ½ lemon
½ cup all-purpose flour
½ cup vegetable oil**

**To serve:
Tartar sauce
Ají amarillo mayonnaise
Plantain chips**

1. Season the fish cubes with salt, pepper, and lemon juice.
2. Dip the fish in the flour, and transfer to a colander to shake the excess.
3. Heat the oil in a frying pan, and fry the fish pieces for about 4–5 minutes. Drain on a paper towel and serve immediately with the sauces and chips on the side.

To make *ají amarillo* mayonnaise, combine ½ cup mayonnaise with 2 tablespoons *ají amarillo* paste, the juice of ½ lemon, and salt to taste. Keep refrigerated up to one day in an airtight container.

SEABASS CHORRILLANA-STYLE

Serves 2

Chorrillos is a traditional fishermen´s district in Lima. Every day, these strong and brave men sail before dawn in search of their daily fish, and then spend the day selling their treasure in the market. Their women are experts at cooking fish and seafood, and most sell *cebiche* and other dishes—such as this one—which are prepared with professional skill.

½ cup vegetable oil
2 garlic cloves, chopped
1 red onion, cut in thick slices
1 tablespoon *ají amarillo* paste
  (optional)
1 tomato, peeled and chopped
½ teaspoon dried oregano
¼ cup red wine vinegar
Salt and pepper
½ cup fish stock
2 tomatoes, peeled and cut in thick
  slices
2 seabass fillets (about 8 ounces each)
2 cilantro sprigs
2 cups cooked white rice

1. Heat the oil in a saucepan over medium heat; add the garlic, and onion, and sauté until transparent.
2. Add the *ají amarillo* paste, chopped tomato, oregano, salt, and pepper. Stir and add the vinegar and stock. Sauté for 30 seconds.
3. Add the sliced tomato and sauté quickly. This sauce should be ready in about 45 seconds or so, if your stove has a strong flame.
4. Meanwhile, season the fish with salt and pepper, and pan fry in a little oil over high heat, until golden on both sides (about 2 minutes on each side).
5. Put a little sauce with veggies on each dish, and top with one fish. Cover with more sauce and veggies, and garnish with a cilantro sprig.
6. Serve with white rice on the side.

If you like fiery food, add more chili pepper to this recipe. You can also leave it completely out if you have a sensitive palate. Serve fluffy white rice on the side, and/or boiled corn, fried sweet potatoes, or steamed yucca.

PAN CON PEJERREY—SMELT SANDWICH

Serves 6

Pejerrey—"smelt" in English—is a small silver fish (about 6 inches long), found in many places around the world, and easily caught in the cold waters off the Peruvian coast. This is a poor man´s delicacy, not only nutritious but also full of flavor. We like to use it in many recipes, from *cebiches* to sandwiches like this one.

1 pound smelts, cleaned and boned
Salt and pepper
2 eggs, lightly beaten
1 cup all-purpose flour
Vegetable oil for frying
 (about ¾ cup)
6 bread rolls (French bread,
 ciabatta, etc.)
½ cup mayonnaise
2 tablespoons *ají amarillo* paste
6 lettuce leaves
***Salsa criolla* (p. 79)**

A word of advice: always buy smelts that have been already cleaned, because they have lots of tiny bones, and cleaning them yourself is a real nightmare.

1. Wash and dry the fish, and season with salt and pepper.
2. Put the lightly beaten eggs in one bowl, and the flour in another one, season with a pinch of salt and pepper.
3. Heat the oil in a skillet over medium heat.
4. Dip each fish in the beaten egg, and then in the seasoned flour, shaking the excess flour off.
5. Fry the fish on both sides, (about 2 minutes per side). Do not overcook. Transfer to a plate covered with paper towels to drain the excess oil.
6. Slice the bread in half, and spread one side with a mixture of mayonnaise and *ají amarillo* paste.
7. Add a lettuce leaf, place three or four fried smelts over the lettuce, and top with *salsa criolla*.
8. Serve immediately.

JALEA

Serves 6

Jalea is simple and delicious. To make it you can use fish, seafood, or both. The contrasting textures of the crispy plantains and the tender fish and seafood is one of the things I enjoy the most about this dish, as well as the citrusy and spicy sauces that complement them.

10 ounces fish fillets
10 ounces squid cut in rings
10 ounces shrimp, cleaned
Salt and pepper
1 cup all-purpose flour or rice flour
1 ½ cups vegetable oil, divided
2 green plantains, peeled and thinly
**   sliced**
3 garlic cloves, finely chopped
1 onion, finely sliced
1 tablespoon cilantro leaves,
**   chopped**
⅓ cup red or orange bell pepper,
**   cut in thin slices**
6 limes, divided
½ cup *ají amarillo* paste
2 scallions, chopped
Juice of ½ lemon
Mayonnaise

Jalea can be served as an entrée or as a shared appetizer, always accompanied by several sauces, thin yucca chips, and *cancha* (Andean popcorn, p. 25). Tartar sauce, mayonnaise, *ají amarillo* sauce, and *rocoto* sauce are just a few of the options you can offer.

1. Cut the fish in 1½ x 1½–inch squares. Season fish and seafood with salt and pepper, and dredge in the flour.
2. Put in a colander and shake the excess flour.
3. Heat 1 cup vegetable oil in a saucepan over medium heat. When hot, add the seafood in batches and cook until golden. Transfer to a plate covered with paper towels.
4. Heat ½ cup vegetable oil in another saucepan, until very hot. Fry the plantain slices until they turn a lightly golden color.
5. To make the onion salsa: Combine the garlic, onion, cilantro, bell pepper, salt, and pepper in a bowl. Add the juice of 2 limes.
6. To make the *ají amarillo* sauce: Combine the *ají amarillo* paste, scallions, and juice of ½ lemon in a bowl, and season with salt.
7. Combine the seafood with fried plantains in a dish, and serve accompanied with the onion sauce, mayonnaise, *ají amarillo* sauce, and lime slices.

SALMON ANTICUCHOS WITH ORIENTAL SAUCE

Serves 4

Asian flavors are deeply rooted in Peruvian cuisine. We love to use exotic ingredients to make sauces and to season many dishes, and *anticuchos* are an example of this. When you make this recipe, you can use shrimp, chicken, or pork instead of salmon.

½ tablespoon sesame seeds
1 pound salmon fillets, cut in
   1 x 1–inch cubes
1 red bell pepper, cut in 1-inch
   cubes
12 scallions (the white part)
½ cup rice vinegar
¼ cup sugar
¼ cup oyster sauce
2 cups fish stock
1–2 tablespoons *ají panca* paste
Salt and pepper
3 tablespoons butter
2 tablespoons scallions (green part
   only), finely sliced

Grilled veggies or vegetable stir-fried rice are a great side for these kebabs.

1. Put the sesame seeds in a pan over medium-low heat, and shake the pan until the seeds become fragrant. Don't do this for too long because they burn fast.
2. Using bamboo skewers, pierce the salmon pieces, alternating with bell peppers and scallions.
3. Put in a dish, season with salt and pepper, cover with plastic film, and refrigerate while you make the sauce.
4. Cook the rice vinegar and sugar in a saucepan over medium heat, until the sugar melts and starts to turn lightly golden.
5. Add the oyster sauce, fish stock, and *ají panca*. Bring to a boil and reduce by half. Season with salt and pepper.
6. Turn the heat to low and add the butter, piece by piece, swirling the sauce in the pan until it's slightly thick and glossy.
7. Grill—or broil—the kebabs for 3 minutes on each side. Do not let the fish dry.
8. Distribute the skewers on 4 plates and cover with the sauce. Sprinkle with sliced scallion greens, the sesame seeds, and serve.

SEAFOOD GRATIN

Makes 1

This dish is one of the stars of the Peruvian restaurant Roberto Cuadra, in El Salvador. It is made to order, with a side of white rice to mop up the delicious sauce.

1 tablespoon butter
1 tablespoon roasted garlic
1 tablespoon *ají amarillo* paste
4 ounces fish, cut in bite-size
   pieces
2 ounces shrimp, cleaned and
   peeled
2 ounces calamari, cleaned and cut
   into rings
2 ounces scallops, cleaned
½ cup white wine
½ cup heavy cream
Salt and pepper
¼ cup mozzarella cheese, grated
2 tablespoons Parmesan cheese,
   grated

1. Turn on the broiler.
2. Melt the butter in a skillet over medium heat. Add the roasted garlic and *ají amarillo* paste, and cook for 2 minutes, stirring.
3. Add the fish, shrimp, calamari, and scallops, and simmer for one minute.
4. Add the white wine, put the lid on and cook for two minutes more.
5. Add the heavy cream, stir, and season with salt and pepper.
6. Transfer to a baking dish, cover with the cheeses, and broil until they are bubbling and golden brown.
7. Serve immediately.

When buying fish, select the catch of the day, and make sure you choose sustainable species only. You can use any variety of fish for most recipes.

GRILLED SEAFOOD WITH SPICY ANTICUCHO SAUCE

Serves 4

The traditional *anticucho* sauce perfectly complements all the fresh seafood in this rustic dish. An ideal accompaniment for it are golden potato slices and boiled corn.

1 small octopus
2 bay leaves
Salt and pepper
1 medium potato
8 ounces calamari, cut in rings
8 ounces shrimp, cleaned
8 ounces scallops, cleaned
2 tablespoons *ají panca* paste
3 garlic cloves, mashed
1 tablespoon paprika
1 teaspoon dried oregano
½ cup olive oil
½ cup red wine vinegar

You can serve this dish in the form of *anticuchos* (kebabs). You can also make it just with fish, or just with one kind of seafood if you prefer.

1. To cook the octopus, add water, bay leaves, and salt to a saucepan and bring to a boil. Holding the octopus by the head, dip the tip of the tentacles in the boiling water. They will curl immediately. Place the octopus in the saucepan, add the potato, and cook. When the potato is tender, the octopus will be tender too. Transfer to a chopping board and let cool to room temperature.

2. Cut the octopus in ½-inch slices and combine with the calamari, shrimp, and scallops in a bowl. Season with salt and pepper.

3. In another bowl, combine the *ají panca* paste, garlic, paprika, dried oregano, olive oil, red wine vinegar, salt, and pepper. Add this sauce to the seafood and mix well. This can be covered and refrigerated for up to 30 minutes before cooking.

4. Heat a griddle over medium-high heat. Add the seafood and cook for about 4 minutes, turning once, or until the shrimp turn pink and the scallops look opaque.

5. Serve at once.

FISH WITH BLACK OLIVE SAUCE

Serves 4

Pulpo al olivo is a famous appetizer consisting of sliced cooked octopus served with a creamy black olive sauce. That was my inspiration to create this dish made with fish fillets instead.

4 fish fillets (about 1-inch thick)
Salt and pepper
Juice of ½ lemon
4 tablespoons vegetable oil
½ cup mayonnaise
¾ cup Botija or Alfonso olives
1–2 tablespoons *ají amarillo* paste
2 cups cherry tomatoes, halved
1 garlic clove, grated
**2 tablespoons fresh oregano leaves
  (or 1 teaspoon dried)**
2 tablespoons olive oil
2 tablespoons lemon juice
**½ cup sunflower sprouts (or any
  other sprouts)**

1. Season the fish fillets with salt, pepper, and lemon juice.
2. Heat the vegetable oil in a skillet over medium heat and fry the fillets until they have a beautiful brown color and are cooked through but not dry.
3. In the meantime, make the olive sauce by processing the olives, mayonnaise, and *ají amarillo,* if using, in a blender until smooth. Reserve.
4. To make the salad, combine the cherry tomatoes with grated garlic, oregano leaves, olive oil, lemon juice, salt, and pepper. Stir and reserve.
5. Put some black olive cream on each plate, and top with a fish fillet, tomato salad, and a few sprouts.
6. Serve immediately.

You can use any kind of fish you like to make this dish. Instead of the tomato salad, you may serve it with steamed potatoes or rice.

CRUNCHY QUINOA SHRIMP WITH SWEET POTATO TRIGOTTO AND PASSION FRUIT GLAZE

Serves 4

Ximena Llosa is a dear friend of ours, and one of the most creative cooks we know. She contributes at Peru Delights and writes the popular blog ximenallosachef.blogspot.com, and is the chef of one of the top TV shows in Peru. This super busy mother of three also works as a caterer and a cooking instructor in Lima, and on top of that, she had time to create a scrumptious recipe using her favorite Peruvian ingredients for this book!

Crunchy shrimp:
20 medium-sized shrimp
Salt and pepper
2 eggs
2 tablespoons *ají amarillo* paste
½ cup flour
¾ cup panko
½ cup cooked quinoa
¾ cup vegetable oil for deep-frying the shrimp

Caramelized sweet potatoes:
2 medium sweet potatoes
4 tablespoons brown sugar
1½ cup freshly squeezed orange juice
2 tablespoons butter
Salt

We love to make risotto using Peruvian cereals. This recipe calls for barley, what we know as *trigo morón*. The name *trigotto* comes from the combination of this grain (*trigo*), and *risotto*. If quinoa is the cereal used, it's called *quinotto*.

Trigotto:
3 tablespoons olive oil
1 small leek, finely chopped
1 medium onion, finely chopped
2 garlic cloves, finely chopped
1½ cup pearled barley cooked for 30
   minutes in salted water (reserve this
   water)
¼ cup white wine
1 cup evaporated milk

½ cup Parmesan cheese, finely grated
1 cup frozen peas,
16 green asparagus, cooked (optional)
Edible flowers, to garnish (optional)

Passion fruit glaze:
1 cup passion fruit juice concentrate
¼ cup brown sugar
1 teaspoon butter

1. For the crunchy quinoa shrimp, start by peeling, cleaning, and deveining the shrimp. Wash in cold water and dry with paper towels. Season with salt and pepper.
2. In a small bowl, whisk the egg with the *ají amarillo* paste.
3. Place the flour in one bowl and the panko and quinoa in another bowl. Coat each shrimp with some flour, removing the excess. Then dip in the egg mixture, and finally coat with panko and quinoa, shaking to remove the excess.
4. Heat the oil in a pan over medium heat and deep-fry the shrimp until they are golden brown and crispy. Transfer to a plate covered with paper towels to drain the oil.
5. For the caramelized sweet potatoes, wash and peel the sweet potatoes, and cut them in ½-inch squares. Put in a saucepan with the other ingredients and cook over medium-low heat until the liquid has a syrupy texture. Swirl the pan until the sweet potatoes are cooked through and caramelized.
6. To make the *trigotto*, heat the olive oil in a saucepan over medium heat. Add the leeks and onion, turn the heat to low, and cook for 15 minutes, stirring frequently. Add the garlic and cook for 2 more minutes.
7. Add the barley and mix well. Add the white wine, bring to a boil, and let it evaporate. Then add the water you used to cook the barley, and cook at medium heat for 15 minutes, stirring constantly.
8. Add the milk and cook over low heat for 5 minutes. Then add the salt and cheese.
9. Before serving, add the sweet peas and the caramelized sweet potatoes.
10. For the passion fruit glaze, put the passion fruit juice and sugar in a casserole, and cook until it is slightly thick, (about 12 minutes over medium heat). Add the butter, turn off the heat, and stir. It will thicken more as it cools down.
11. Serve the *trigotto* on 4 plates.
12. Place the shrimp on top and garnish with some green asparagus and a few edible flowers.
13. Finish with a tablespoon of passion fruit glaze on the sides.

SUDADO

Serves 4

Here you have a variation of *sudado*, a traditional dish from the northern coast of Peru, where it is cooked with *chicha de jora*, and served with seafood, boiled yucca, or rice. A nice and creamy lima bean puree is also a good side dish.

2 tablespoons vegetable oil
1 red onion, cut in thin slices
3 garlic cloves, mashed
2 tablespoons *ají amarillo* paste
    (optional)
3 tomatoes, peeled, seeded, and
    grated
1 tablespoon tomato paste
3 cups fish broth
¼ cup white wine
4 cilantro sprigs
Salt and pepper
4 sea bass fillets

1. Heat the oil in a saucepan over medium-high heat. Add onion and garlic, stirring from time to time, and cook for 10 minutes. Add *ají amarillo* paste, tomato, and tomato paste, stirring constantly.
2. Incorporate fish stock, white wine, and the cilantro sprigs, cover the pan, lower the heat, and cook for 15 minutes. Season with salt and pepper.
3. Season the fish fillets and put in the saucepan. Put the lid on and steam the fish in the flavorful broth until the fillets look barely opaque. Be careful and do not overcook them.
4. Serve one piece of fish on each plate, surrounded with the sauce.

Sudados are full of flavor and light, perfect if you want to lose some unwanted pounds.

SOMETHING SWEET

SUSPIRO LIMEÑO

Serves 4

In her fabulous cookbook *El Perú y sus Manjares*, Jossie Sisson de De la Guerra narrates the story of this silky dessert, crediting the poet José Gálvez with its peculiar name. Apparently, this artist was a romantic even when it came to the food he ate, comparing this pudding to the gentle and sweet sigh of a girl from Lima. Yes, *suspiro* means "sigh."

1 12-ounce can evaporated milk
1 14-ounce can condensed milk
3 eggs
1 cup sugar
¼ cup port wine
3 tablespoons water
Ground cinnamon, to garnish

For the whites to grow the way they should, they must have no trace of egg yolk, and the bowl must be spotlessly clean and completely dry. Even the slightest residue will change the result.

1. Cook the evaporated milk and the sweetened condensed milk in a heavy-bottomed saucepan over medium heat, stirring constantly with a wooden spoon until the mixture thickens slightly and turns a pretty caramel color, (about 30 minutes). Turn off the heat.
2. Separate the egg whites from the yolks, and use a wire beater to beat the yolks in a small bowl. Add a couple tablespoons of the hot milk mixture and keep beating for a few seconds.
3. Pour the yolks in the pan with the milks, combine carefully, and reserve.
4. Mix the sugar, port wine, and water in another pan. Bring to a boil over high heat, without stirring. The syrup is ready when it forms a caramel thread when poured from a spoon. (230–235°F in a candy thermometer).
5. While the sugar is melting to form the caramel, beat the egg whites using a standing mixer at high speed until soft peaks form (you will know they're ready when you lift one of the beaters and it has a soft cloud of meringue foam around it).
6. Add the hot syrup in a thin, steady stream, beating vigorously until the resulting meringue is completely cold.
7. Pour the cold milk mixture in a large container—or nice glasses. Cover with a large dollop of meringue and dust with a little ground cinnamon.
8. Serve cold, and keep refrigerated.

MAZAMORRA MORADA

Serves 6

This purple dessert is made with the same water used for *chicha morada,* with the addition of dried fruits, sweet potato starch, and extra sugar. You want it to be slightly thick but still runny. If you add more thickener than needed, the texture will resemble gelatin, which is not what we are looking for.

3 pounds purple corn
3 cloves
3 cinnamon sticks
1 pineapple, peeled and chopped
1 Granny Smith apple, peeled and cored
1 quince, peeled, cored, and chopped
9 cups water
½ cup prunes
½ cup dried apricots
½ cup sweet potato starch (or potato starch)
1½ cups sugar
1 lime
Ground cinnamon

I like to add dried cranberries, cherries, and blueberries to this dessert instead of the traditional prunes. Peruvian food purists would never forgive this sin, but I think these fruits enhance the flavor of any *mazamorra morada.*

1. Break the dried corn in several pieces.
2. Put in a heavy saucepan along with the cloves, aniseed, cinnamon sticks, pineapple peels, apple, quince (peel and core included), and water.
3. Bring to a boil over high heat, and cook for 15 minutes. Turn the heat to low and cook partially covered for 1½ hours.
4. Strain, reserving the liquid and discarding the solids.
5. In the same saucepan, put the purple liquid, 2 cups chopped pineapple, chopped apple, prunes, apricots, and sugar. Bring to a boil, turn the heat to medium, and cook for 20 minutes to soften the fruits.
6. In a bowl, dissolve the potato starch in a little water and add to the saucepan, stirring constantly. Cook for 5 more minutes.
7. Turn off the heat, and add the lime juice. Stir.
8. Serve in ramekins or glasses, sprinkled with ground cinnamon.

RICE PUDDING

Makes 6

The Spanish brought sugar, rice, and milk to Peru, along with many recipes for desserts. Rice pudding is one of them, and it's been a staple in every home ever since. Street vendors all over the country sell this comforting and delicious pudding in plastic cups, always warm, especially during the winter.

4 cups whole milk
2 cinnamon sticks
1 cup Arborio rice
2 cups evaporated milk
1 cup water
Peel of 1 lemon
1 cup sugar
1 teaspoon vanilla essence
2 teaspoons ground cinnamon

You can add raisins, dried cherries, or blueberries to the preparation. You can also flavor the pudding with ¼ cup Pisco, rum, Cointreau, or Amaretto, if you are planning on serving it to adults only.

1. Simmer the whole milk with the cinnamon sticks and the rice, in a heavy saucepan over medium heat. Stir the mixture every now and then, and make sure the milk does not boil over or stick to the bottom of the pan.
2. When the rice is tender (about 25–30 minutes), add the evaporated milk, water, sugar, and lemon peel. Continue simmering, stirring with a wooden spoon until it is slightly creamy (about 25 minutes longer).
3. Do not let the pudding dry because the rice will absorb more liquid as it cools, and the mixture will become thicker.
4. Remove from the heat, and discard the lemon peel and cinnamon sticks. Add the vanilla essence and stir.
5. Pour into a nice container, or individual cups or glasses. Dust with ground cinnamon, and serve.
6. It can be refrigerated and served cold as well.

CREMA VOLTEADA—FLAN

Serves 8

Is there a place in the world where this creamy dessert hasn't left its mark? Flan is a sweet way to celebrate everything and nothing at all, and in Peru you can find it wherever you go. We call this vanilla-flavored custard *crema volteada* (literally "upside down cream").

1 cup white sugar
1 14-ounce can sweetened condensed milk
1 12-ounce can evaporated milk
6 eggs
1 teaspoon vanilla essence

To soften the hard caramel that remains at the bottom of the pan after unmolding the flan, put the empty baking pan over medium heat with ⅓ cup of water in it. Stir with a spoon until it becomes liquid again, and pour over the flan.

1. Preheat the oven to 375°F.
2. Heat the sugar in a saucepan over medium-high heat, stirring until it melts and forms a liquid caramel. Be careful not to let it burn because it will taste bitter.
3. Carefully pour the hot caramel into 8 ramekins, rotating them to cover the entire inner surface with the caramel. Be very careful with your fingers, and don´t even dream of tasting it with your tongue. Hot caramel is extremely dangerous.
4. Process the condensed milk, evaporated milk, eggs, and vanilla in a blender. Pour this into the prepared ramekins.
5. Put them inside a larger pan with about 1-inch of hot water.
6. Bake in this water bath for 40 minutes. Take out of the larger pan and transfer to a rack to cool completely.
7. If you have the time, keep refrigerated for several hours (or overnight) to loosen the caramel.
8. When ready to serve, run a knife around the edge of each ramekin, cover with a dish, and turn upside down.
9. Keep refrigerated.
10. You can make this flan in a 9-inch round baking pan, and bake for one hour.

EASY APPLE CAKE

Makes 6

I like to think of this cake as part of my daily fruit portions, because apples are the main ingredient. Some berries can also be added to it, such as blueberries, raspberries, blackberries, or even cranberries.

6 apples (any kind you like)
Grated zest of 1 lime or lemon
1 teaspoon ground cinnamon
1 tablespoon sugar
½ cup blueberries
1 cup light brown sugar
1 cup cake flour
3 eggs
1 cup vegetable oil
1 teaspoon vanilla
2 cups whipped cream or vanilla ice cream
¼ cup blueberries, to decorate

Top with vanilla or berry ice cream for a more stylish presentation.

1. Preheat the oven to 375°F.
2. Peel and core the apples. Cut them in thin slices, put them in a bowl, and sprinkle them with lime or lemon zest. Add the cinnamon and 1 tablespoon sugar, and stir to combine.
3. Put the apple slices in a greased 9-inch baking pan. Add ½ cup blueberries.
4. Put the brown sugar, flour, eggs, vegetable oil, and vanilla in another bowl.
5. Mix with a spatula or a wire whisk, and pour over the apples.
6. Bake for 55 minutes or until golden.
7. Serve warm or at room temperature with whipped cream or ice cream, and a few blueberries.

TRES LECHES

Serves 6

The texture and flavor of this moist cake will improve if you make it in advance and keep it in the fridge. The traditional recipe covers the cake with a meringue layer, but if this is too sweet for you, leave it plain or add some whipped cream and fresh fruit instead. You are going to love it either way.

3 eggs at room temperature
1 cup all-purpose flour
1½ teaspoon baking powder
½ cup sugar
¼ cup milk at room temperature
1 14-ounce can condensed milk
1 12-ounce can evaporated milk
1 cup heavy cream
1 teaspoon vanilla essence

The flavor of this dessert can be custom-made by blending any fruit of your liking into the milk mixture. You can also blend in chocolate or coffee.

Tres *leches* keeps well in the fridge for several days, but make sure you cover it with plastic film to keep it moist.

1. Preheat the oven to 350ºF.
2. Sift the flour together with the baking powder.
3. Beat the eggs at the highest speed for about 5 minutes. They have to grow to about 3 times the volume (or more) from when you started beating them. Make sure your mixer is completely dry before you pour the eggs, otherwise they won´t grow the way they should. Same advice goes for when preparing the meringue.
4. Add the sugar, little by little, while still beating the fluffy eggs.
5. Turn the beater down to slow speed and add a third of the flour, then a third of the milk, then a third of the flour, and so on, until all the ingredients blend completely.
6. Transfer to a 12 x 8–inch baking pan and bake for 30 minutes.
7. In the meantime, mix the 3 milks with the vanilla and set aside.
8. The cake is ready when you pierce with a knife and it comes out clean. Bake for a few minutes longer if necessary.
9. Take the cake out of the oven and pierce it all over with a fork. Pour the cold milks over the cake immediately, so they are absorbed by the hot cake. Make sure you do this evenly and cover every part of the cake, including the sides and corners.
10. Cool and decorate with mango slices and mint leaves. Or put the *tres leches* in the fridge to serve very cold.

CHOCOLATE CAKE

Serves 10–12

I don´t think this rich, fudgy, syrup-drenched cake is originally from Peru. However, it is hugely popular in Lima and you can find it in every bakery, café, corner store, and home. If there's a birthday party, rest assured that this will be the cake holding the candles.

3 cups cake flour
8 tablespoons cacao powder
1 teaspoon instant coffee
1 teaspoon salt
2½ teaspoons baking soda
1 cup vegetable oil
2 cups milk
1 tablespoon vinegar
1 teaspoon vanilla essence
3 eggs
2 cups sugar
**½ cup sliced almonds or coconut
   flakes**

For the syrup:
1 cup water
½ cup sugar
1 teaspoon vanilla

For the fudge:
½ cup cacao powder
3 tablespoons hot water
**1 12-ounce can unsweetened
   evaporated milk**
1 14-ounce can condensed milk
2 tablespoons butter

To make this cake you only need a bowl, a spoon, and a baking pan. This means that you don´t even need a mixer to blend it all together.

1. Grease a 10-inch tube pan, and cover the bottom with parchment paper.
2. Preheat the oven to 350ºF.
3. Sift the flour, cacao coffee, salt, and baking soda, in a big bowl.
4. Make a well in the center and add the oil, milk, vinegar, vanilla, eggs, and sugar. Mix with a spatula or wooden spoon.
5. Pour into the baking pan and bake for 1 hour. Let cool.
6. To make the syrup: Put the water and sugar in a small saucepan. Bring to a boil until the sugar dissolves. Add the vanilla essence and cool.
7. To make the fudge: Stir the cacao into hot water until it dissolves completely. Put the evaporated milk, condensed milk, and cacao in a pan, and cook over medium-low heat, stirring all the time, until the mixture thickens and you can see the bottom of the pan.
8. Turn off the heat and add butter. Stir. If it´s too thick, add a little milk.
9. To assemble the cake: Cut it in three layers and pour some syrup on each one.
10. Spread some fudge on the first layer, and cover with another layer. Repeat.
11. Cover the cake with fudge, and sprinkle with sliced almonds or coconut flakes.

CORN CAKE

Serves 6

The texture of this cake is light and moist, and it has an intense corn flavor. The tiny amount of flour used (only two tablespoons) is enough to bind everything together, making a perfectly formed dessert.

**1 stick unsalted butter
  (about ½ cup)**
½ cup sugar
2 eggs, whites separated
1 egg yolk
**1 package cream cheese, at room
  temperature**
2 cups fresh white corn
2 teaspoons baking powder
2 tablespoons all-purpose flour

We use Peruvian giant kernel corn for this cake, but if you can't find it, any white corn is good. We don´t recommend yellow corn, however, because it is too sweet.

1. Have all the ingredients at room temperature before starting. Line the bottom of a 9-inch round baking pan with parchment paper.
2. Preheat the oven to 350ºF.
3. Beat the butter and sugar until creamy. Add the egg yolks one by one, then the cream cheese. Beat at high speed for 5 minutes.
4. Process the corn in a blender or food processor until very fine. Add to the butter mixture along with the baking powder and flour.
5. Meanwhile, beat the egg whites in the mixer at high speed, until soft peaks form. Fold very gently into the corn mixture, with a spatula.
6. Pour the batter into the pan and bake for 45 minutes or until the cake is lightly golden.
7. Remove the cake from the oven and cool on a rack.

TURRÓN DE CASTAÑAS

Serves 8–10

We call this dessert *turrón* although it has nothing in common with the Spanish *turrón* or the Italian *torrone*. This very sweet cake can have either a chewy or a crunchy texture, depending on how finely or coarsely grated the Brazil nuts are.

4 eggs
2 cups sugar
¾ cup butter, melted
1 cup cake flour
1 teaspoon baking powder
¼ teaspoon salt
2 cups Brazil nuts, grated or finely chopped
2–3 cups *manjar blanco* (dulce de leche)

You can also bake this cake in rectangular baking pans. In this case you will need to adjust the baking time, adding about 10 minutes.

1. Preheat the oven to 350ºF.
2. Oil 2 round 9-inch baking pans, and line them at the bottom with parchment paper. Beat the eggs and sugar with a mixer on medium speed, until light and fluffy. Add the melted butter.
3. Turn the speed to low, and add the flour, baking powder, and salt.
4. Turn off the mixer, and add the grated Brazil nuts, stirring with a spatula.
5. Pour the batter into the pans and bake for 25 minutes.
6. Cool on racks, pass a knife along all the edges of the pan, and unmold. When completely cool, cover one of the cakes with *manjar blanco*.
7. Put the other cake on top, and cover the whole outside surface of the two-layered cake with more *manjar blanco*.
8. To decorate, make lines all over the outer layer of *manjar blanco* with the tines of a fork.

PASSION FRUIT MOUSSE

Serves 6

Passion fruit is a wonderfully versatile fruit that can be used to make juices, desserts, cocktails, and even to add its acidic touch to *cebiches* and savory sauces. This mousse, created by chef Roberto Cuadra, is a great dessert to make whenever you have some free time, and leave in the fridge, ready to be eaten whenever you feel the urge for something sweet.

For the mousse:
1 tablespoon unflavored gelatin
2 tablespoons water
½ cup cream cheese, at room temperature
1 14-ounce can sweetened condensed milk
1 cup heavy cream, cold
8 ounces passion fruit juice

For the topping:
½ tablespoon unflavored gelatin
2 tablespoons water
2 ounces passion fruit juice
2 tablespoons sugar

To garnish (optional):
Mint leaves
Maraschino cherries

You can also serve this dessert with whipped cream and/ or strawberry sauce. To make the sauce, process 2 cups strawberries with 2 tablespoons sugar and the juice of ½ lime, in a blender. Strain and refrigerate until ready to serve.

1. To make the mousse, mix the unflavored gelatin with 2 tablespoons cold water, and rehydrate for 5 minutes. When it blooms, melt in a saucepan over very low heat, stirring constantly, until it dissolves. Set aside to cool.
2. Beat the cream cheese and condensed milk using a mixer, until very creamy. Add the heavy cream and continue beating for three minutes. Then add the passion fruit juice and the melted and cooled gelatin. Pour this mixture into 6 glasses, and refrigerate for at least 4 hours.
3. In the meantime, make the topping by mixing the unflavored gelatin with 2 tablespoons water, and letting it rehydrate for 5 minutes. Bring the passion fruit juice and sugar to a boil, in a saucepan over medium heat. Add the rehydrated gelatin and heat until dissolved. Cool to room temperature and pour over the firm mousse. Refrigerate until ready to serve.
4. Serve with a cherry and a couple of mint leaves (optional).

QUESO HELADO

Serves 15

Arequipa is the birthplace of this sweet artisanal ice. This recipe was given to us by celebrity chef Blanca Chávez, author of the beautiful cookbook *Entre Hornos y Rocotos*.

4 cups milk
2 cinnamon sticks
4 cloves
1 cup sugar
2 ounces dried coconut, grated
1 tablespoon vanilla
1 teaspoon cornstarch
5 egg yolks
1 12-ounce can unsweetened
  evaporated milk
1 14-ounce can sweetened
  condensed milk
Ground cinnamon

1. Bring the milk to a boil in a heavy saucepan over high heat, with the cinnamon sticks, cloves, sugar, and grated coconut. Turn the heat off immediately.
2. Drain and discard the spices, add the vanilla, and the cornstarch (previously dissolved in a little water). Let it cool.
3. Process the egg yolks in a blender with the unsweetened evaporated milk. Add this to the spiced milk and stir in the sweetened condensed milk.
4. Pour into a container and put in the freezer for several hours. Once frozen, cut in squares or serve with a scoop, and sprinkle with ground cinnamon.

Originally, this dessert was made with almonds, but eventually people started using coconut because it was cheaper and more accessible.

BAVAROIS DE GUINDONES

Serves 8–10

We call this light dessert *merengón*, which means "large meringue." This baked meringue studded with chopped prunes, and covered with caramel—just like flan—is always served with custard on the side.

1 cup sugar
¼ cup water
6 eggs, whites and yolks separated
14 tablespoons sugar, divided
1 cup prunes, chopped
1 12-ounce can unsweetened
   evaporated milk
1 teaspoon vanilla essence
8–10 whole prunes for garnishing

Instead of prunes, you can use any dried fruit to make this dessert. Dried pears, figs, apricots, or raisins, are a few good choices.

1. Preheat the oven to 350°F.
2. To make the caramel: Put 1 cup sugar and ¼ cup water in a heavy saucepan, bring to a boil, stirring until all the sugar has dissolved. Continue cooking undisturbed until golden. Pour into an 11-inch tube, moving it so it covers the whole inner surface of the pan. Be careful because it will be very hot. Reserve.
3. In the bowl of a mixer, beat the egg whites at high speed until soft peaks form. Add 10 tablespoons sugar, beating continuously. Turn off the mixer.
4. Using a spatula, fold the chopped prunes into the meringue. Pour into the prepared baking pan, and put this pan in a larger pan with about 1 inch of boiling water. Bake in this water bath for 50 minutes.
5. Take out of the oven, let cool, and then refrigerate without unmolding. You can bake it one day in advance and keep it in the fridge.
6. While the *bavarois* is in the oven, prepare the custard by beating the egg yolks and remaining 4 tablespoons sugar with a wire whisk. Do this vigorously until it becomes light and pale (about 3 minutes).
7. Add the evaporated milk, transfer to a pan, and cook over very low heat, stirring constantly with a spatula or wooden spoon, until lightly thickened. Take off the heat and cool. Strain and transfer to a jar or bowl, and keep refrigerated.
8. To serve, unmold the *bavarois*, by running a knife along the edge of the pan, putting a plate on top, and turning it upside down.
9. Serve it with a little of the residual caramel sauce in the pan, and with custard. Garnish with a prune.

CORNSTARCH ALFAJORES

Makes 35

Alfajores are a sweet treat that has been present all over Latin America since colonial times. Each country has a different way of preparing alfajores, but the concept is the same: two cookies filled with dulce de leche. This is Antonella Delfino's family recipe.

4 egg yolks
4 tablespoons sugar
⅔ cup unsalted butter, at room temperature
2 cups cornstarch, sifted
4 teaspoons baking powder
2 tablespoons fresh milk (if needed)
1 14-ounce can dulce de leche
Confectioners sugar, for dusting

You can bake the cookies in advance and store in a tightly sealed jar or tin for up to 5 days. Fill them with dulce de leche right before serving.

Serve *alfajores* with a glass of milk, with coffee or tea, or even with ice cream.

1. Preheat the oven to 350°F.
2. Beat the egg yolks with the sugar in a mixer, for 3 minutes at medium speed. Add the butter and continue beating until creamy.
3. Add the cornstarch and baking powder in three parts, mixing them in with a spatula, and then knead lightly with your hands until the dough is no longer sticky. If the dough feels dry add the milk.
4. On a floured table, roll the dough with a floured rolling pin to make a thin layer of about ⅛-inch thick.
5. To make the cookies, cut the dough with round 2-inch cookie cutters. Prick all over with the tines of a fork, and bake for 8 minutes on baking sheets covered with Silpat or parchment.
6. If you don't have cookie cutters, be creative. You can use the top of a glass or cup, which will make slightly larger *alfajores*.
7. Cool the cookies on racks. When completely cool, put a teaspoon of dulce de leche on half of them, and place another cookie on top, like a sandwich. Sift confectioners sugar over them. You can even make three-layer *alfajores* to serve with ice cream.

PANETÓN WITH ICE CREAM

Makes 4

When my kids were growing up, they loved the many desserts I made using the traditional Christmas *panetón* (this is what we call the Italian *panettone*). Sometimes it was bread pudding, others it was French toast, but their favorite thing was to have mini *panetones* filled with ice cream. They are very easy to make and can be frozen for months, so Christmas can last for the whole year.

2 mini *panettone*
2 cups ice cream
1 cup blackberries

You can easily find different kinds of mini *panettone* in many grocery stores. Fill them with whipped cream or pastry cream instead of the ice cream if your prefer.

1. Cut off the top of each *panetón*.
2. Make a hole in the center, pulling out some of the crumbs from the middle.
3. Combine the ice cream with blackberries, mashing the fruit.
4. Fill each *panetón* with ice cream. Put the top back on and wrap them in foil.
5. Freeze and use as needed.
6. Before serving, transfer to the fridge for 15 minutes. Discard the foil and cut in half.
7. Keep frozen for up to 3 months.

CHAMPUZ

Serves 10

This traditional dessert from Lima shares its funny name (it sounds like *shampoo*), with a local fruit. Originally, it was served as a hot beverage during cold winter nights. During the Spanish Colonial period, it was typical to hear the *champuceras* (women who prepared and sold *champuz* on the streets) announcing their product.

8 ounces *mote* (hominy)
½ pineapple, peeled and chopped
1 cup sugar
2 cinnamon sticks
4 cloves
2 Granny Smith apples, chopped
1 quince, peeled and chopped
½ cup corn flour
1 soursop (*guanábana*), peeled, seeded, and chopped
Ground cinnamon

The usual fruit used to make this recipe is soursop, which is similar to cherimoya, but less sweet. The latter could be a good substitute if soursop is not available. We added apples to this recipe, even though it´s usually made just with pineapple, quince, and soursop.

1. Soak the *mote* overnight, in a bowl full of water. You can even soak it for 2 days, changing the water a couple times, to soften the *mote* even more.
2. Drain, change the water, and cook partially covered, until the *mote* is soft. This may take about 2 hours. Turn off the heat, drain, and reserve.
3. Put the pineapple, sugar, cinnamon sticks, and cloves in another saucepan filled with boiling water. Simmer for 15 minutes over medium heat.
4. Add the apples and quince, and cook for another 15 minutes.
5. Put the corn flour in a bowl, and add a little water. Mix until the flour is completely dissolved and without lumps. Add to the saucepan where the fruit is cooking, together with the soursop (*guanábana*) and the cooked *mote*, and cook for 5 extra minutes, stirring frequently.
6. Serve in tall glasses, warm or at room temperature, and sprinkled with ground cinnamon.
7. You can also put it in the refrigerator once it has cooled, and warm it again before eating.

KIWICHA AND CHERRY BROWNIES

Makes 10–12

If you´ve never used the highly nutritious Andean seed known as amaranth (we call it *kiwicha*), this is your chance to experiment with it. The texture is a cross between quinoa and cooked oatmeal. Try it in these perfectly gooey brownies, and see how you feel about it. I´m sure it will be love at first bite.

½ **cup butter (melted)**
1 **cup Turbinado raw sugar**
2 **eggs**
¼ **cup whole wheat flour**
¼ **cup almond flour**
¼ **cup cooked amaranth**
¼ **teaspoon Peruvian pink salt (or any other salt)**
⅓ **cup cacao powder**
¾ **cup fresh cherries (pitted and coarsely chopped)**

Turn these brownies gluten-free by substituting the whole wheat flour with half almond flour and half cooked amaranth.

1. Preheat the oven to 350ºF.
2. Grease and flour a 8 x 8–inch baking pan.
3. Mix the butter and sugar in a bowl.
4. Add the eggs and beat with a fork or a hand whisk.
5. Add the dry ingredients (whole wheat flour, almond flour, salt, and cacao powder), and the cooked amaranth, and whisk until you have a smooth batter. Stir in the cherries.
6. Pour the batter into the baking pan, and bake for 30 minutes.
7. Let it cool on a rack for half an hour or longer.
8. To unmold, pass a knife through the inner edges of the pan, put a large dish or baking tray on top, and turn over. Tap the pan strongly on all sides to loosen it.
9. Cut in equal portions and serve immediately or store for up to 2 days in an airtight container, separated with parchment paper.

BRAZIL NUT BALLS

Makes 48

One or two of these tiny treats look beautiful next to a steaming cup of tea of coffee. They will make your friends feel special when they visit you, or make you look extra professional and meticulous if used at business meetings.

2 14-ounce cans condensed milk
3 egg yolks
2½ cups Brazil nuts, coarsely
  grated and divided

These candies can be made up to 4 days in advance, and they will actually improve in flavor as the days go by. Keep them in tightly sealed containers at room temperature or in the fridge.

1. Cook the condensed milk, eggs yolks, and 2 cups Brazil nuts, in a heavy saucepan over medium heat. Stir frequently until you can see the bottom of the pan.
2. Turn off the heat and transfer to an oiled plate. Cool completely.
3. Toast the remaining ½ cup Brazil nuts in a clean skillet, stirring until lightly golden and fragrant.
4. When the milk and nut mixture is cool, put a little vegetable oil in your hands, and form balls with ¾ teaspoon of the mixture. Roll the little balls on the toasted Brazil nuts until completely covered.
5. Put in candy paper cups and serve.

MINI VOLADORES

Makes 40

Light, sweet, and pretty . . . these *voladores* are the mini version of the *volador*, a dessert that has been popular in Lima for over a century. The trick to make them is to roll the dough until very thin—almost transparent—and then prick it all over with the tines of a fork, baking it until cooked but still pale in color.

1 cup all-purpose flour
Pinch of salt
6 egg yolks
3 tablespoons Pisco
½ cup *manjar blanco* (dulce de leche)
½ cup pineapple marmalade (or any other flavor)
½ cup confectioners sugar

These cookies, made with the same dough used for *guargüeros*, are served with coffee or tea at many social gatherings and celebrations. You can use the same dough to make a large *volador*, the size of a regular cake.

1. Sift the flour and salt. Put them on the table and make a well in the center.
2. Add the yolks and Pisco to the well. Using your fingers, start to incorporate the flour with the yolks and Pisco, until a dough is formed.
3. Knead with your hands until the dough is elastic and doesn´t stick to your fingers. Form a ball, cover with plastic wrap or put in a plastic bag, and rest at room temperature for about 20 minutes.
4. Preheat the oven to 350°F.
5. Sprinkle the table with flour. Take a small portion of the dough (about ½ cup) and roll with a rolling pin until very thin. You should be patient and keep rolling, until you get a perfect, smooth layer. Cut in 1-inch circles.
6. Place them on a baking sheet covered with parchment or Silpat, and prick each one several times with the tines of a fork. Repeat with the rest of the dough.
7. Bake for 8 minutes, until firm but not golden. Cool on wire racks.
8. Place one layer of cookies on a plate, and put ½ teaspoon *manjar blanco* or dulce de leche on each one. Cover with another cookie. Place ½ teaspoon pineapple marmalade, and top with a third cookie.
9. Sift confectioners sugar over them.
10. Place each volador in a paper candy cup, and serve.

GUARGÜEROS

Makes 36

What can you make with flour, salt, egg yolks, and Pisco? The answer is this versatile dough used to make fried *guargüeros* and also baked *voladores*. In Lima you can buy these lovely cookies in many bakeries, grocery stores, and coffee shops, but there is something rewarding—and relaxing—about making them yourself.

1 cup all-purpose flour
⅓ teaspoon salt
6 egg yolks
¼ cup Pisco
2 cups vegetable oil
1–2 cups *manjar blanco* (dulce de leche)
½ cup confectioners sugar

In Peru many people make *manjar blanco* (Peruvian dulce de leche) at home for this recipe and many others. We, however, don't recommend this, as it is very time consuming, and your sweet tooth will not like the wait! Just buy dulce de leche at the store (it needs to be the thick kind, not runny), and use this.

1. Sift the flour and salt. Put on a table and make a well in the center.
2. Add the egg yolks and Pisco in the middle. With your fingers, start to incorporate the flour with the yolks and Pisco, until a dough is formed.
3. Knead with your hands until the dough is elastic and doesn´t stick to your fingers. Form a ball, cover with plastic wrap or put in a plastic bag, and rest at room temperature for about 20 minutes.
4. Sprinkle the table with flour. Take a small portion of the dough (about ½ a cup) and roll with a rolling pin until very thin. You should be patient and keep rolling, until you get a perfect, smooth layer. Cut in 2-inch squares per side.
5. Place an egg white drop in one of the corners and fold, pressing the moist corner against the opposite corner.
6. Heat the oil in a small saucepan over medium heat.
7. When hot, fry the guargüeros for 2–3 minutes. They will float when they are ready. Do not let them brown.
8. Transfer to a plate or a wire rack covered with paper towels, and let them cool.
9. Put the *manjar blanco* or dulce de leche in a piping bag with a rosette tip, and fill the *guargüeros*.
10. Sift confectioners sugar over them and serve.
11. You can make the cookies in advance and keep them in a sealed container for up to 2 days. Fill them with *manjar blanco* when ready to serve.

AGUAYMANTO COOKIES

Makes 7

My daughter created this recipe for Christmas a few years ago. These cookies are unique, with the texture of the dried *aguaymantos* (golden berries or pichuberries) and the grown-up flavor of Pisco. I like to freeze the raw balls of dough for up to several months, and only bake one or two when I have a craving.

½ cup light brown sugar
¼ cup sugar
1 stick unsalted butter, softened
1 egg
1 tablespoon Pisco
1¼ cup all-purpose flour
½ teaspoon baking soda
½ teaspoon salt
25 dried *aguaymantos* (pichuberries or golden berries), macerated overnight (or up to 3 days) in Pisco
2 ounces pecans, chopped

If you don´t want to use Pisco in this recipe, substitute with 1 teaspoon vanilla essence. Instead of aguaymantos you can use raisins, dried cherries, or dried cranberries.

1. Mix the sugar, brown sugar, and butter in a bowl, with a wire whisk. Add the egg and Pisco.
2. Incorporate the flour, baking soda, and salt. Then add the macerated *aguaymantos*, previously drained, and the pecans.
3. Form 2-inch balls with an ice cream scoop, and put them on a baking sheet covered with silpat or parchment.
4. Put in the fridge for a couple of hours, or freeze them to bake later.
5. Preheat the oven to 375°F. Bake the cookies for 10–12 minutes.
6. If frozen, do not thaw, but bake for 15 minutes.

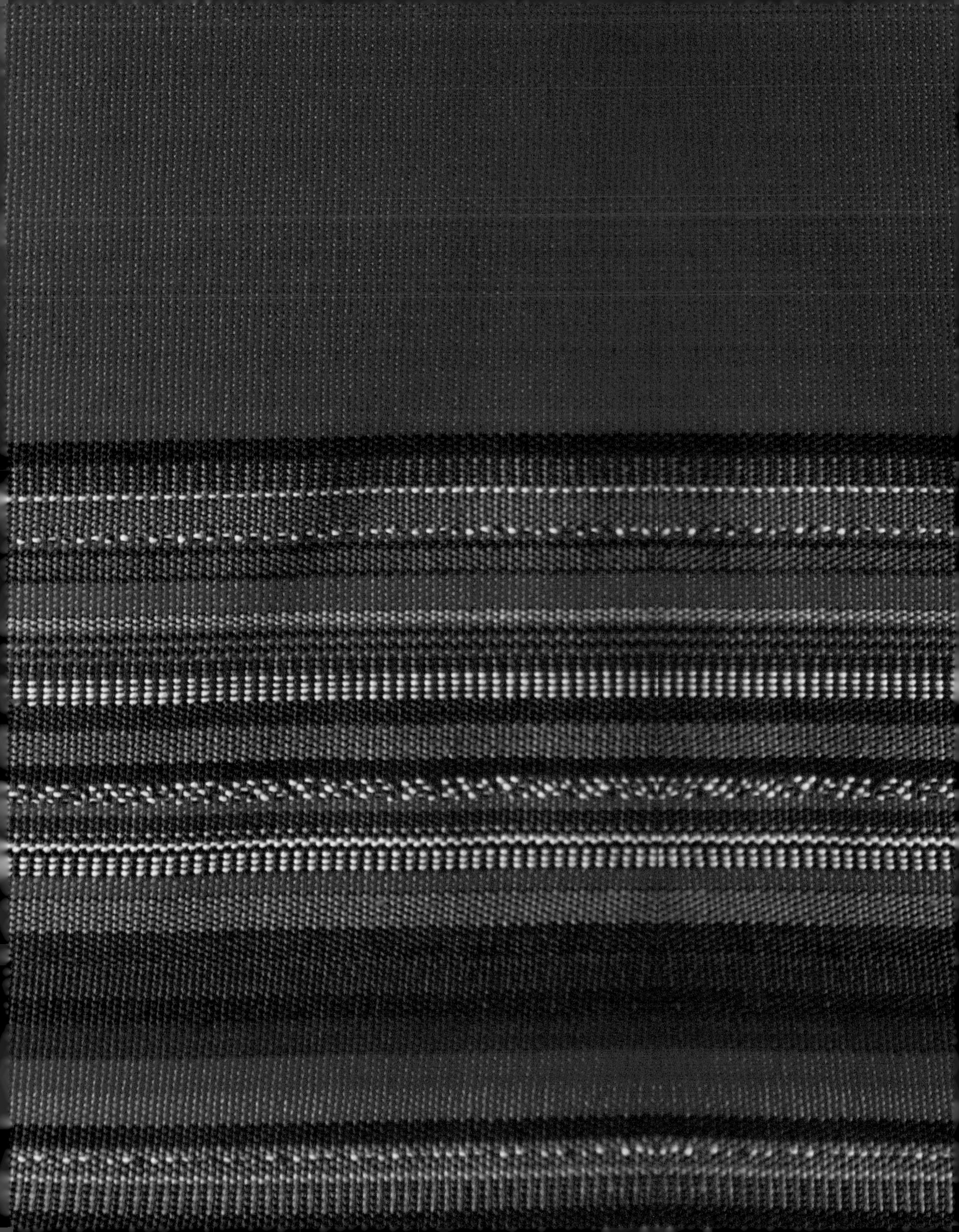

DRINKS

CHICHA MORADA

Serves 6

The perfume of apple and pineapple in this deep purple drink always makes me think of dessert. Drink it whenever you're thirsty, as it's not only delicious and refreshing, but it also possesses great diuretic properties, and is especially beneficial for people with high blood pressure.

2 pounds purple corn
Peel of 1 pineapple
2 Granny Smith apples, coarsely
   chopped
1 quince, coarsely chopped
2 cinnamon sticks
6 allspice berries
6 cloves
12 cups water
Sugar to taste
Juice of 3 limes

1. Put the purple corn, pineapple peels, apples, quince, cinnamon sticks, allspice, cloves, and water in a large saucepan. Bring to a boil, lower the heat, and simmer for about an hour, partially covered. The water will turn a deep and vibrant purple color. Turn off the heat and cool.
2. Strain, discarding the solids. Add sugar to taste and the lime juice.
3. Serve very cold.

The popularity of purple corn is mostly due to being the main ingredient in this beverage, and in *mazamorra morada*, one of our staple desserts. Nowadays you can find it in many health food stores in the form of flour, to be used for baking and other preparations.

PISCO SOUR

Serves 3

There are dozens of stories about the origin of this popular cocktail, but most connoisseurs agree that it was first made at the Morris Bar, in Lima, in the early 1900s. This place was very famous for the quality of its Pisco Sours and the buzz it gave its drinkers.

9 ounces Pisco
3 ounces lime juice
4½ ounces simple syrup
8 ice cubes
1 egg white, lightly beaten
3 drops Angostura bitters

1. Process the Pisco, lime juice, simple syrup, ice cubes, and egg white in a blender until frothy.
2. Serve in a glass and add a drop of Angostura bitters.

To make simple syrup at home, boil a cup of water with a cup of sugar for 5 minutes, stirring until the sugar is completely dissolved. When it cools down, put it in a bottle and keep refrigerated for up to 2 months.

FROZEN PASSION FRUIT SOUR

Serves 1

Passion fruit juice gives this cocktail a stunning orange color and a floral flavor. If you freeze it before using, you can turn this into an irresistible popsicle, ideal for the summer.

3 ounces unsweetened passion fruit juice (this is usually sold frozen in many supermarkets)
1 ounce Pisco
1 ounce simple syrup
10 ice cubes

1. Process all the ingredients in a blender until smooth.
2. Serve immediately.

To make fresh passion fruit juice, cut the fruit in half and put the pulp in a blender, process at low speed for 15 seconds strain, discarding the seeds.

CHICHA MORADA SOUR

Serves 1

In recent years different versions of *Pisco Sour* have become the darlings of Lima's nightlife. Most of them use native fruits and leaves, and this one has the bright purple *chicha morada* as its main ingredient, injecting some spiciness into the traditional sour.

2 ounces *chicha morada*, unsweetened (p. 227)
1 ounce lime juice
1 ounce simple syrup
3 ounces Pisco
5 ice cubes

1. Put the *chicha morada*, lime juice, simple syrup, Pisco, and ice cubes in a cocktail shaker.
2. Shake and strain into a nice glass.
3. Serve immediately.

You can make a simple *chicha morada* for this cocktail by boiling 1 pound purple corn in 6 cups water, with a pineapple peel, an apple cut in thick chunks, 2 cinnamon sticks, 4 cloves, and 4 allspice. Cook for 45 minutes, and then strain it and continue boiling for an extra 15 minutes to concentrate the flavors.

ALGARROBINA

Makes 1

This sweet and creamy cocktail is considered a girly drink by many men. It is usually enjoyed before a meal, as an aperitif.

3 ounces Pisco
2½ ounces *algarrobina*
   (or carob syrup)
2 ounces unsweetened evaporated
   milk
1 egg yolk
4 ice cubes
Dash of ground cinnamon

1. Mix the Pisco, *algarrobina*, evaporated milk, egg yolk, and ice cubes in a blender and process until smooth.
2. Serve and dust with ground cinnamon.

For an even creamier and sweeter cocktail, add 1 ounce condensed milk to the preparation. Your sweet tooth will be pleased.

CHILCANO

Makes 1

If you visit one of the oldest bars in Lima, called *Antigua Taberna Queirolo*, you will find the best *chilcanos* and *butifarras* in town. This is not a fancy place, but it offers a wonderful array of Pisco cocktails and infusions.

2 ounces Pisco
¼ ounce lime juice
1 glass ginger ale, icy cold
1 lime slice
Dash of bitters

1. Put the Pisco and lime juice in a tall glass. Add the ginger ale and stir.
2. Add ice cubes and a slice of lime. Finally, add a dash of bitters and serve.

Sprite, 7Up, or any other clear soft drink can be used instead of ginger ale. When using dark soda, the cocktail takes the name of *Peru Libre*, our version of the famous *Cuba Libre* made with rum and Coke.

PISCOPOLITAN

Makes 1

The classic Cosmopolitan has been recreated with the addition of Pisco, becoming one of the easiest Peruvian cocktails to make at home. This is a great drink to serve with *tequeños* or any other hors d'oeuvre.

2 ounces Pisco
1¼ ounces lemon juice
1¼ ounces cranberry juice
¾ ounce Cointreau
5 ice cubes
1 Maraschino cherry (optional)
1 lemon slice (optional)

1. Mix the Pisco, lemon juice, cranberry juice, Cointreau, and ice in a cocktail shaker.
2. Shake and serve in a cold glass, garnish with a cherry and lemon slice.

Pisco comes in different types: *Quebranta, Italia, Acholado*, and *Mosto Verde*. *Quebranta* and *Acholado* are the most neutral of these, so we recommend them when making cocktails. Stronger, more fragrant Piscos will overpower the flavor of most cocktails.

GLOSSARY

TUBERS

Mashua

Similar in looks, but not as popular as potatoes, mashua is considered the antidote for an overindulgent sex drive (yes, there is an antidote for that!). It can be eaten on its own, or as part of many dishes, by roasting it, mashing it, or adding it to many sweets and desserts. An easy way of enjoying its sweet side is roasting it and serving it with honey. Its neutral flavor also makes it the ideal side dish. When they want to use this tuber, Andeans put it in the sun for a day or two to bring out all its best qualities.

Oca

This tuber is sweet, especially if kept in the sun for a couple days before cooking, just like mashua. Its starch content is low, giving it a less floury texture than potatoes, and it is so versatile that it can be used in sweet or savory dishes alike. You can make a gratin with layers of oca and other tubers, or mash it instead of potatoes whenever you want a comforting meal.

Olluco

This Andean tuber looks like a small, finger-shaped potato, with colors that range from pale to bright yellow, to orange, pink, and red. It has a somewhat slimy and watery texture, very different from the starchy and doughy characteristics of a potato, and it can be eaten raw or cooked, and always unpeeled (just scrub it under running water and cut it in fine sticks or round slices). The preferred way of cooking it is in stews and *chupes* (thick soups). Of these stews, ollucos with *charqui*—dried llama meat—is far and away the most popular. The name of this ingredient comes from the Quechua word *ullucu*, which means "tuber." It is also called *papalisa* (smooth potato).

Sweet Potato

Delicious and nourishing, the sugar content of this tuber makes it extremely sweet and energizing. Sweet potatoes also help regulate high blood pressure, and are fantastic to relieve stress. One inch of sweet potato added to juices will give you bright and shiny hair. You can find white, purple, and orange varieties, but Peruvians love the sweeter orange ones to serve next to a fresh *cebiche*, or thinly sliced, fried, and stacked inside a *pan con chicharrón* (pork sandwich).

Maca

Maca is a root, sometimes considered a tuber, and it belongs to the carrot family. It is known as the "Peruvian ginseng" for its energizing properties. Maca increases the body's resistance to stress, trauma, and fatigue, and boosts sexual function (this is the reason why it's also known as the Inca's Viagra). It is also popular to relieve depression and anxiety, and brighten your general mood. Use it sparingly in juices and smoothies because its strong flavor can be overpowering (one teaspoon a day is a good dose to start). If you happen to find fresh maca, make sure you cook it before using it. To do this, you first need to peel it, and finely chop it or grate it, and then cook it in boiling water until soft (about 30 minutes).

POTATOES

Potato

This is one of the stars of Peru's rich soils, as our country boasts over three thousand types of potatoes. Carb haters may have given it a bad reputation in the past few years, but Peruvians have been thriving on this tuber since ancient times. Potatoes are a great source of vitamins and minerals, and they are also rich in iron, antioxidants, fiber, potassium, and magnesium. One tablespoon of raw potato juice before breakfast is a great way to calm gastritis and rheumatism, and folk medicine claims that the water in which potatoes have cooked is good to relieve kidney pain and to prevent kidney stones.

Papa Seca

Drying potatoes is an ancient technique that is still in use to preserve these crops. Incas were so efficient at growing potatoes that they dried and stored the surplus, eradicating famines from their culture, as papa seca was always in stock. The drying method consists of cooking potatoes in boiling water, peeling them, and cutting them in medium-sized cubes or thin sticks. Then these pieces are sun-dried until they lose all their moisture and look like small crystals. After this process they are ready to be stored for a long time (more than a year).

When buying papa seca choose the ones with a yellowish color, believed to be of better quality than the transparent or brown ones. You can buy them in bulk at any Peruvian market, or in grocery stores where they are sold already packed. Store them at room temperature.

Papa seca is the main ingredient of a famous dish called *Carapulcra*, but sometimes a mix of fresh and dried potatoes is used to make it. This sturdy entrée is made with pork and chocolate, and is accompanied by a side dish called *Sopa Seca*, which means "dry soup," made with noodles.

Chuño

This name comes from the Quechua *ch'uñu*, which literally means "freeze-dried potato." Chuño is made with regular potatoes that are dried in the heights of the Andes. The word also refers to a very fine potato starch made with the same freeze-dried potatoes, which are commonly used to thicken sauces and desserts such as *Mazamorra Morada*.

There is white and black chuño. The latter is made with bitter potatoes, which are left to freeze overnight in the open air. In the morning, they thaw under the sun, and then they are crushed to extract their liquid, and frozen all over again at night. This process is repeated many times until the potato is completely dehydrated.

To make white chuño, on the other hand, potatoes are soaked in the icy cold water of rivers and streams for several days, and then sun-dried.

Chuño has an extremely long shelf life (it lasts for several years), and it has been part of the Andean diet for centuries. To consume it, you need to rehydrate it by soaking it in water. It is mainly used to make Andean soups and stews, or you can just cook it and eat it with corn and cheese.

CORN

Choclo

We call it *choclo,* and it has been one of the main staples of Peru's daily diet for thousands of years. There are dozens of varieties in every color and size imaginable, but the most used has giant, meaty kernels (about the size of a thumb fingernail or bigger) that are full of crunch. With choclo we make tamales, cakes, breads, and soups, or we eat them boiled or roasted, accompanied by big chunks of salty *queso fresco* and *ají* sauce. When boiling corn, we add a couple tablespoons of sugar to the water and an aniseed teabag. A few drops of lime juice is optional if you want to keep the kernels pearly white.

Mote

Giant kernel corn is boiled with wood ashes or slaked lime to peel the kernels. This process is known as nixtamalization in Mexico. Then the kernels are peeled and dried and used in several Andean savory dishes, and in some desserts like *champuz*. It's very similar to hominy (you can replace it with it), and it can also be eaten cooked and accompanied with some artisan cheese.

Purple Corn

This is one of the many varieties of corn native to Peru. It has gained status as a superfood thanks to its diuretic effect and its incredible antioxidant content, which gives it its intense purple color. Sold dried and by the kilo, purple corn is the main ingredient of the refreshing drink called *chicha morada,* and of the traditional dessert with Arab roots known as *Mazamorra Morada.*

To use purple corn you usually make purple water, and then use that water in your cooking. To do this, take the kernels off the cob first, but don´t you dare discard the cobs because that is where the secret lies: the cobs render even more color than the kernels! Add both cobs and kernels to a large pan with apples, quince, pineapple peels, cinnamon sticks, cloves, and allspice, cover with water and bring to a boil until the water has a deep purple color (about 45 minutes). Cool and strain, discarding the solids. With this water you can make a unique purple rice that will have a beautiful color and also a fruity and spicy flavor.

Cancha

Different varieties of dried corn (*chulpe* is one of them) are used to make the Andean version of popcorn called *cancha.* Don't expect anything like the popcorn you're used to eating at the cinema (which, by the way, is called *canchita* in Peru). These corn kernels are toasted in a clay pot with or without oil, and as soon as they start to crack open, salt is added to them. The result is a crunchy, starchy, golden kernel that is served at the table to nibble on before a meal, and that is highly addictive!

AJÍ

Ají Amarillo

Chili peppers are native to the Andes. Ancient Peruvians relied on salt, herbs, and *ají* as seasonings, and when the pre-Hispanic man wanted to offer a sacrifice to the gods, he fasted avoiding *ají*, salt, and sex for a few days. *Ají amarillo* has a crisp texture, paired with a floral aroma and a bright orange color (despite being called yellow chili pepper). As long as you remove the veins and seeds, it can be eaten cooked or raw. In fact, raw sliced or blended *ají amarillo* is the base for many of our traditional dishes. Strangely, this chili pepper has several names, and none of them is a true description of it: *ají escabeche*, *ají amarillo* (yellow chili pepper), and *ají verde* (green chili pepper).

Ají Limo

This chili pepper comes in a rainbow of colors: red, orange, yellow, green, white, and purple. It is used both to add a colorful note to many dishes, and to spice them up as well. *Ají limo* is a medium-sized pepper (about 2 or 3 inches long), and it is one of the oldest and hottest found in Peru. Some people say that it stores most of its heat in the tip, but beware of the seeds and ribs too! *Ají limo* is usually eaten raw, and is a must in *cebiches* and *tiraditos*. Nowadays you can find *ají limo* paste in Latin American grocery stores all around the world.

Ají Mirasol

This is a sun-dried chili pepper with a unique earthy flavor and intensity. It is less floral and citric than fresh *ají amarillo*, but has a more complex and concentrated taste that goes well with soups and stews. Seed and devein it first, toast it in a dry pan over medium heat until fragrant, and then blanch it in boiling water, changing the water three times to reduce its heat. Some brave people like to deep-fry the whole pepper until golden brown, and serve it over bean stews or *chupes* (Andean soups).

Ají Panca

Another basic ingredient in countless Peruvian recipes, this sun-dried chili pepper has a brick red color, and a smoked aroma and flavor that brings depth to many slow-cooked dishes. It is also sold as *ají especial* (special chili pepper), or *ají colorado* (red chili pepper).

Rocoto

This is one of the hottest chili peppers from Peru, despite its innocent appearance, which is very similar to a bell pepper. Rocoto is mainly used raw as a condiment, adding just a small amount to some dishes to give them a fiery kick.

SEEDS

Kiwicha (Amaranth)

With tiny seeds smaller than quinoa, this is an ancient and nutritious American crop, known and consumed in Mexico and Peru. It was banned by the Conquistadors—just like quinoa—because they attributed magical powers to it, claiming it was used for witchcraft. Nowadays, it is found as amaranth in many international stores. You can use it in similar ways as quinoa, but keep in mind that *kiwicha* is smaller, takes a bit longer to cook, and has a slightly sticky texture that is terrific for making healthy puddings.

Quinoa

Chances are you are familiar with quinoa by now (pronounced *keen-wah*), or have heard of its nutrient-dense properties. "A complete protein" is what we've heard the most when it comes to this powerhouse, and indeed it is a complete protein, as it contains all the essential amino acids, on top of iron, calcium, vitamins E and B. What very few people know is that despite being treated as a cereal, this wonderful ingredient is not a grain, but technically a seed. We learned this from a friend whose glucose was alarmingly high and was prohibited to consume any sugars or grains by her Chinese medicine homeopath. She broke the wonderful news: quinoa was not on the forbidden list.

This superfood has been a staple of the Andean diet throughout the centuries, and it grows high in the mountains despite the cold weather. The Incas considered it sacred because it provided them with energy and good health, and they loved to offer it to their gods.

VEGETABLES

Caigua

This Quechua name means "cucumber," and the seeds of this fruit have been found in ancient tombs dating back to 3700 BC. Caiguas are like green capsules filled with black seeds and a hairy vein. They can be eaten raw (in salads), or stuffed with meat, fish, chicken, or vegetables and served with rice on the side. Legend has it that the bitter juice of this vegetable aids in losing weight and lowering high cholesterol levels. Adding the juice of half a lemon will make it palatable and easier to drink.

Loche Squash

This beautiful squash also goes by the names of *lacayote, avinca*, and simply *zapallo* (squash). It comes from the northern coast of Peru and has been widely used in the gastronomy of this part of the country since pre-Columbian times. The flowers and the fruit are used both in savory and sweet dishes. *Loches* are very pretty too, sometimes resembling swans or ducks. This squash is indispensable when making northern dishes like rice with duck.

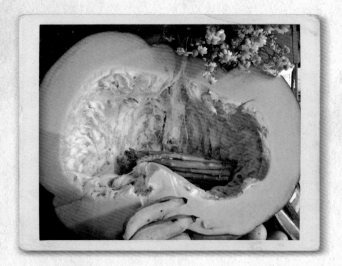

Macre Squash

This squash is the most popular in Peruvian cooking. It is one of the largest in the world, with more than one hundred pounds of golden-orange pulp. We use it for *locros,* soups, purees, and even to make risotto or fill many types of pasta. It makes a delicious sweet as well, cooked in molasses syrup.

FRUITS

Aguaymantos (Golden berries)

They look like tiny yellow tomatillos covered with papery husks, but have a juicy pulp full of miniature seeds. These berries are a lovely addition to salads, yogurt, juices, shakes, and desserts. Their delicate sweet and sour flavor is also fantastic when cooked in sweet or savory sauces. If you're a vegetarian, you will be happy to learn that this fruit is considered a superfood thanks to its high content of many nutrients, including vitamin B12, iron, and protein.

Camu Camu

This small round fruit grows wild in the Peruvian and Brazilian rain forests, and it resembles a large grape with green, red, and yellow colors fused together. Camu camu has big seeds and a juicy pulp, and it is considered the richest source of vitamin C in the world, and as such, a superfood. It is unlikely that you will find the fresh fruit in markets or grocery stores outside of Peru, but dried camu camu powder is sold as a nutritional supplement in many health food stores and in some regular grocery stores.

Cocona

This bright orange berry is the size of a large avocado, looks like a conic tomato when cut in half, and has a very acidic flavor. Originally from the Amazon jungle, it's one of the favorite ingredients of the local cuisine, and widely consumed in the form of spicy sauces, juices, nectars, ice cream, popsicles, and desserts.

Consume *cocona* only when very ripe. You will know it is ready when the skin begins to wrinkle.

Granadillas

They belong to the passion fruit family but have a very delicate and sweet flavor, far from the acidity of passion fruits. The color of their juice is different as well—nearly transparent—nothing in common with the intense orange or yellow of their cousins. This juice is so sweet and mild, that in Peru it is the first fruit juice given to babies after breast milk (an ounce or so at mid-morning is energizing and they love it). To make it, place the pulp of some granadillas in a sieve and press with the back of a spoon to release the juice contained around each seed.

You can also eat granadillas just as they are. Their pulp is soothing for the stomach, the liver, and the nervous system. All you have to do is cut the hard peel in half with a knife or with your fingers, and eat it with a spoon.

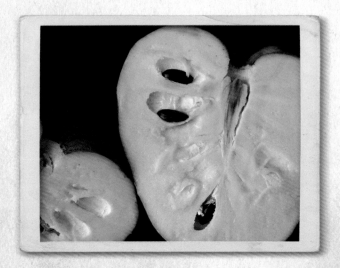

Cherimoya

This name is a Quechua word meaning "cold seeds." Cherimoya is so sweet and creamy that we highly recommend eating it on its own as a dessert, with no further embellishments. This fruit can be used in desserts, ice creams, cakes, juices, and smoothies. To eat, make sure it's soft on the outside, and then proceed to peel the fruit and discard the black seeds, which are inedible.

Limes

Asian in origin, this crop came to Peru via the Spanish colonizers, and adapted itself to the soil and climate of Northern Peru. Our variety—we call it *limón sutil* (subtle lemon)—is smaller than others and has an intense acidity, perfect to marinate the raw fish used to make *cebiche*. To get the best of its juice, it should be squeezed with a gentle hand, just enough to get the juice out without the bitter oil from the skin.

Lúcuma

There is nothing like fresh lúcuma to make desserts and shakes. Its pulp has a beautiful orange color, with a characteristic fragrance similar to the Mexican and Central American *zapote*; but its texture has nothing in common with this tropical fruit, being creamy and starchy instead of juicy. You will know a lúcuma is ripe when the skin starts to burst open. Discard the large seeds, and process the pulp to use in any recipe you want (desserts love it!).

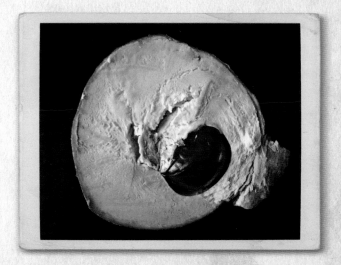

Maracuyá (Passion Fruit)

Like most Peruvians, we love the acidic flavor and floral fragrance of this fruit, and as a bonus, its flower is one of the most beautiful things we have ever seen in nature. This is not a taste to be enjoyed on its own, but it is ideal to flavor beverages, nectars, desserts, and sweet and savory sauces. The variety of passion fruit we find in Peruvian markets is yellow and heavy for its size, because the pulp is full of seeds and juice. Buy them when they are plump and the skin is starting to show wrinkles. To juice them, strain the seeds by putting the pulp in a sieve and pressing with a spoon to release the liquid. You can also process it in the blender with quick pulses or at low speed to avoid grounding the seeds, which should be discarded before using.

Sachatomate

Its name is Quechua and means "tree tomato," but in other parts of the world it is known as *tamarillo*. It is very similar to a tomato both in flavor and texture, and there are a few varieties of it in Peru. We like to enjoy them in spicy sauces, desserts, and compotes. Sachatomates can be eaten raw or lightly cooked.

Tumbo

This fruit looks different from its relatives, passion fruit and *granadilla*. Tumbo has an oval shape, and ranges in size from about five inches long, to the giant variety of the Amazon that weighs more than five pounds. Its skin has the same yellowish color of passion fruit, but it is softer. Cut lengthwise or crosswise, you will find hundreds of black seeds, each surrounded by a bubble of orange, tart juice. This is used to make refreshments, desserts, and ices.

Tomatoes

Surprise, surprise! This fruit, consumed as a vegetable, is native to Peru, and didn't spread to the rest of the world until just a few hundred years ago. As a matter of fact, when tomatoes were first brought to Europe, they were considered potentially dangerous, and for many years were used only as decoration. No one could imagine the rave tomatoes were going to cause in the world´s gastronomy once people warmed up to their versatile taste.

OTHERS

Sacha Inchi

This is an Amazonian legume very similar to a peanut. It can be eaten like a snack (we love it covered in chocolate), but the most common presentation nowadays is in the form of oil. This oil is a healing potion for the body, considered one of the world's most powerful superfoods because of its high levels of antioxidants and essential fatty acids. One tablespoon a day in your salad dressing is enough to get all the healthy fats your body needs to stay in top shape.

Recently discovered by scientists, sacha inchi helps lower blood pressure, strengthens the immune system, has large amounts of vitamins A and E, lowers cholesterol levels, and is good for the digestive system, for the brain, and for the bones.

Be careful when adding it to salads, shakes, or other preparations, because it has a very strong flavor that some describe as fish like, and can take some getting used to.

Huacatay (Black Mint)

This is a popular herb used in many Peruvian dishes—mostly in the Andes—which imparts its characteristic pungent flavor to many soups and stews. It is hard to think of a delicious *locro*, or a creamy *ocopa* sauce without the sharp taste of this herb. You can also enhance a simple *ají* sauce with just a few chopped huacatay leaves or a teaspoon of huacatay paste.

This aromatic leaf is also called "black mint" because it is part of the same family of herbs. Just like mint, it's better to use it sparingly, as it has a pungent taste that can easily become overpowering.

It's not easy to find fresh huacatay outside of Peru, but you can easily buy it in paste form over the Internet and use this instead. Start with a little bit and increase the amount according to your taste.

Sal de Maras (Peruvian Pink Salt)

In the valley leading to the lost city of the Incas, a unique salt harvest has taken place for 2,000 years. Like a vast marble staircase, about 4,200 terraces of salt tumble down the hillside toward the town. There are green, ochre, gray, white, and pink pools filled with this first-grade salt ready to be harvested. These healthy and nutritious pink crystals help stabilize and regulate heartbeat thanks to their sodium and magnesium content.

Cilantro

Also known as coriander, cilantro is one of the many herbs that came to Peru from other parts of the world. It contains many vitamins and minerals, promotes good digestion, and is a powerfully detoxifying herb. In Peru we only use the leaves, which are basic in soups like *aguadito*, in many rice dishes, in stews like *seco*, and to make a certain kind of tamales called *tamalitos verdes* (small green tamales). Store it in a plastic bag in the fridge, or keep it in a glass of water with the roots inside the water.

RECIPE INDEX